BEERVANGELIST'S™
Guide to the Galaxy

By Fred Bueltmann

Black Lake Press
TELL YOUR STORY
BLACKLAKEPRESS.COM

Photography by Jeff Hage, Green Frog Photo.
General editorial, cover, and interior design by Greg Smith.
Illustrations and cover art by Jessica Newton and Sarah Brummels.
Published by Black Lake Press of Holland, Michigan.

Black Lake Press is a division of
Black Lake Studio, LLC.
Direct inquiries to Black Lake Press at
www.blacklakepress.com
ISBN 978-0-9883373-6-7

Dedication

Mom and Dad

You have always encouraged me to believe that I can.

I am forever grateful for the amazing patience you showed while I struggled to figure out how.

Ulla

Cooking for you is one of my life's greatest pleasures.

Table of Contents

Recipes

Acknowledgements

Ulla: your love and support makes this all possible.

Jeff Hage and Green Frog Photo, along with Joanie Homrich: your generous spirit, eyes, and perspective bring artistry and beauty to these pages and to the world.

My New Holland Brewing Company family: our camaraderie and shared vision is incredibly inspiring and rewarding.

Greg Smith and the team at Black Lake Studio & Press, including Cory, Sarah, and Jami: your coaching, expertise, and patience were invaluable and encouraging.

Mom, Dad, and Family: you have been there through it all.

Chef collaborators, including St. Anthony's Matthew Millar, Food Dance's Robb Hammond, Salt of the Earth's Matthew Pietsch, and Publican's Paul Kahan and Brian Huston.

Everyone I've worked with, especially in the beer and spirits world and the Michigan Brewers Guild: you are a beautiful and motley crew that inspires me regularly. Julie Stanley at Food Dance: you admirably brought food with integrity to the table, well before many people knew they wanted it. The cooking party gang on "The Hill," Amy, Matt, Heather, Roberta, and Penny. Ray Daniels, Garrett Oliver, Stephen Beaumont, and Lucy Saunders: for whetting my appetite with early influence on presenting beer and food. The gang at Food for Thought Magazine, especially Mindy Simon and Sue Osgood. Kristen Tracy: for your genuine and generous encouragement and counsel. Mark, Matt, Casey, and the crew at "my local," Salt of the Earth in Fennvile, Michigan: it's hard to tell what's more fun, eating at Salt, or cooking there. Robin Langer: for the cozy writing cave. Suzanne Huffman: you always knew I would do it. Linda Murray: the energy you brought to teaching lasts a very long time. Betsy Leonard Haage and Carolyn Christofani: I owe you dinner.

Thank you to my wonderfully supportive, confidence-building Kickstarters, including Greg Bueltmann, the Gary Family, Beau's All Natural Brewing Co., Chris Black, Jim Brown, Kurt R. Jensen, Brian Evenson, and Kristen Tracy.

Foreword

Before Fred and his wife Ulla moved to Fennville, I would look out to the east of my home and see a dilapidated farmhouse slouched on thirty neglected acres of pasture and orchard. Not so long after, fences were mended, gardens planted, the house became warm and inviting, and the beginnings of a neighborhood I take great pride in being a part of started to take shape. Our two households share a common love for the provenance of the food and drink we consume. As a result, the last several years have seen us gardening, canning and pickling, raising and butchering hogs, and breaking bread, lighting fires, and mixing cocktails together.

We have a rural lifestyle that I think many people would envy. This is in large part because Fred and Ulla share their farm and its facilities generously. But also because Fred is willing to take on new challenges without hesitation if it involves something he has real passion for, especially in the kitchen. Fred is largely a self-taught cook, and this can be a very tricky way to learn. When you are without a mentor, learning to cook is full of pitfalls and uncorrected misdirection. Fred was able to overcome much of this because he did something smart from the very beginning: he trained his palate.

I tell my young cooks that it is just as important to learn to eat as it is to cook. The palate is a culinary muscle, and like any other it needs to be developed and challenged to become strong. It's exercise that includes the brain, and if you don't develop it diligently, all the culinary technique in the world will never make you a good cook. It seems like Fred understood this intuitively from the very beginning. Maybe his background in beer was the primary driver, but I would imagine once Fred started thinking critically about beer, food wasn't far behind.

Fred always took on cooking with a genuine desire to do it right and come away from his experiences in the kitchen with tangible knowhow. He is not afraid to jump headfirst into deep water, and when he comes out, he no longer lacks the expertise I sometimes worried he had too little regard for going in. For Fred, the unknown is a bonanza of discoverable knowledge and a storehouse of skills that are just there waiting for those with the tenacity to reach out and tackle them.

This is one of the main reasons I have been very excited to read this book. Fred's enthusiasm doesn't tire easily, so over the course of his experiences he has gained quite a wealth of knowledge. He came by these new skills through hard work and respect. His story and the voice he uses to tell it are very much his own. He understands that to be larger than life, one must absorb as much life as possible and share it with the world generously, honestly, and with integrity. If you open yourself up to it, it is unlikely that you will experience the world of food, drink, and entertaining the same way after getting a glimpse at it through Fred's eyes. More importantly, you may be moved to put your doubts and timidity aside and tackle some herculean, harebrained scheme that, once mastered, will enhance the quality of your everyday life, and perhaps even leave you with a few stories of your own to tell. I know this is one of the legacies of my friendship with Fred that I have come to cherish. I am glad to see the world will get an opportunity to know it for themselves.

Matthew Millar, Chef

James Beard Foundation Semifinalist, Best Chef Great Lakes 2011, 2012 James Beard Foundation Semifinalist, Best Chef Great Lakes 2011, 2012

Author's Note

It's easier than ever to take a chance on picking a new beer, or finding an old favorite. With a few broad-stroke pointers and a little encouragement to keep it simple, I hope you enjoy the company of good friends, good drink, and good food. You'll find that Beervangelist's Guide to the Galaxy is not an encyclopedic guide to styles, stats, or information on brewing of beer. Instead, it's a casual invitation to taste for yourself. I believe finding a beer to enjoy is neither complicated nor difficult.

For a career beer guy, there is an awful lot of food in this book. I've wanted to share my passion for cooking and pairing for a long time, and I wrote this with everyone from the novice to the industry professional in mind. Most specifically, though, I wrote it for the home cook, host, and entertainer.

In some small way, I'm inviting you all into my home, as the remarkable photography of Jeff Hage brings you there. Most of the food in this book was cooked in my home while feeding friends, and Jeff beautifully captured the essence of it all beautifully.

This book is written from my personal perspective, although you'll notice plenty of references to New Holland Brewing Company. I know our beers intimately, as I'm grateful to serve as one of the managing partners of the brewery, along with Brett and Dave. The recipes and pairings are designed to help you find your next beer no matter where you are or whose beer you're drinking.

The world is in our glass and on our plate.

Enjoy!

Spring

Opening Salvo

I get a lot of comments about the title "Beervangelist" on my business card, a title that has become my moniker in the industry. It makes me happy, because I get to reply to the question, "What does a Beervangelist do?" My standing answer, "I bring beer to the people," is met with chuckles, "Amen," and "Preach on!" I give you that it's a lighthearted mission—I mean, c'mon, who wouldn't love that job? I'm also quite serious, as I believe that beer is the most underrated beverage in the history of the world.

I've decided to write this "Guide to the Galaxy" because I have been fortunate enough to travel, along with my many colleagues, deep inside the world of beer, enjoying immense vistas of intrigue and flavor. There's something else, though. Along the way, my idea of flavor changed entirely. I started looking at it differently, less technically and more as a sensory memory captured and saved by my palate. I found myself explaining beer and brewing to people using all sorts of analogies to help it all make sense to them. What was at first a method of explanation became a new way of thinking. This is especially valuable when selecting beers for people or for a plate of food. I have always respected and developed an understanding of the technical side of things, but my instinctive and sensory awareness is what leads me.

I've always loved beer. However, when my relationship with food and cooking developed, I began to pair intuitively, and boy howdy, shit started to change. You can feel it when flavors intersect. Instead of thinking about it intellectually, deciding whether you agree with the pairing or not, certain moments just take over. You might lose your breath, hear yourself moan a little into a sigh, or perhaps your head drops back while you exhale.

Alright, you perverts, I recognize that it sounds like I just described an orgasm. You know what? They're not that far apart. Sex and combining flavors have a lot in common; mostly, you know the difference between when it's deeply personal and when it's mechanical. It's difficult to list or describe, but you know it when you feel it, and when it's good... you want to do it again.

Learning to pair beer and food intuitively and mindfully has been a series of tuning-fork moments for me. I've felt my palate, mind, and body reverberate with sensation as flavors meld. I feel as if I've discovered paths and trails that few get to visit. There are some spots I've visited over and over again, showing everyone I can, something that I know they need to see. There are some places to which I only take solid travel companions who are ready for adventure and challenge. There are some amazing and well-documented milestones from my travels. Others might be random stops, repeated only if I stumble upon them again and feel the wash of familiarity telling me, "I've been here before..."

I want visitors to become guests and guests to become regulars. But in a weird sort of way, like a cryptic Lynch-esque character at the trailhead, I want to tell you there are no rules... except don't forget the rules. By now, I'm sure you think I've broken a rule already and eaten the brown acid, but I promise that if you join me, we'll find some shit you've never imagined possible.

Beervangelist's Rules
of Galactic Travel

Listen to Your Palate, Your Brain is a Liar
Honor Ingredients, Use Technique

It's Not About You
You're Not Alone
Flavor First

Mindfulness, Above All Else

You'll hear me talk about mindfulness a lot. To me, mindfulness is taking a moment to stop and think about "what am I looking for?" If you stop to ask a question, to consider what you have and what you want, you'll likely find yourself making better choices.

Throughout this book, I'm going to encourage great choices. We're in the midst of a flavor renaissance in both beer and food. We're taking back our industry and supply chain from monolithic giants that took away our choices. We are still on the early edge of sea change, but, as they say, "the tides have turned."

The thing is, there is a duality to my Beervangelism. On one hand, I want to rally us all to stand tall and shout in a strong voice for change. I want the world to be on notice that we're tired of the bullshit and that we care about what we eat and drink, and who makes it.

On the other hand, at the core of my philosophy is that people should eat and drink whatever the hell they want. Quality and pleasure are most abundant when choices feel easy and natural, not forced or coerced.

My objective is to help make it easier and easier. I'll share some stories that hopefully shed a little light on why and how I made changes in my life. I'll suggest things for you to think about when choosing what you eat and drink. I stay pretty true to my flavor-first mantra, but there's a little soapbox-standing mixed in for good measure.

Making it easy is not only the target—it's also what fuels change. It's an interesting chicken-and-egg cycle. The more people who support a way of life, the stronger the supply chain gets. The stronger the supply chain gets, the easier it is for more people to come on board.

Take a look at the beer shelves in almost every beer or grocery store in America and you'll see real change. Ten years ago there were certain chains and stores that just didn't carry craft beers. They weren't "in," and, therefore, not a viable option. For some people, they still aren't, but the choice to enjoy craft beers has never been easier, and that is a sign of huge progress.

It ends up being about choices. When there's an abundance, choosing can be overwhelming. How do you pick a beer when there are thousands staring back at you? When there are limited or poor choices, it's about carving out an alternative. If you want a better choice than what is available, you have to either change the place you shop, or change the way you shop; otherwise, you'll have to settle for less.

There is a time and place for everything. I'm sharing with you my ideals and the successes and failures I've enjoyed while shooting for them. While some of the approaches, techniques, or even objectives of the lifestyle in this book may seem daunting to some, they're old hat to others. I set my course to care about what I eat and drink and to celebrate that, as living beings, we may be the only species to not only prepare food but also to prioritize flavor right along with nutrition and sustenance.

While it wouldn't be out of context to hear "Ale-eluia!" or "Preach on!" at a Beervangelist's beer dinner, I want to be clear that Beervangelism does not include elitist judgment. I am inviting you to check out these ideas as you'd like and when you can, because I think you'll enjoy them.

In the end, this is not an all-or-nothing proposition. Whether you're already "in" or just testing the waters, I hope there's something here for you. Feel free to use what makes sense and enjoy what suits you. I encourage patience, creative problem solving and, above all, mindfulness.

If I help you pause for a moment, consider your options, and make a choice that's good for you and your guests, that's good enough for me.

Inspired to Entertain

Having people over to my place was one of the first thrills of living on my own. I lived in a dorm during my first year of college, and we managed to create a series of parties orchestrated around turning our two-room suite into a party den for an evening. One of my suite mates and I had something in common: the instinct to turn a party into an experience. The event I remember the most was the "Reggae Bash." We cut out magazine letters and images to create the invitation at least a week in advance. We even slipped the invite into our music professor's stack of homework assignments to pseudo-invite him. We moved all of the furniture from one room to the other, making an open, loft-like floor plan out of room 503 before such arrangements ever came into vogue. We set punch bowls made from converted Rubbermaid tubs in the bathtub and surrounded them with ice. We filled the punch bowls with fruit punch, orange juice, vodka, oranges, and Lord knows what else. A stack of CDs and cassettes of reggae were cued up, the tie-dyes were donned, and voila, a reggae party was born.

The following year, I moved into my first apartment, and the theme events continued. I believe I held the 2nd Annual "Halloween Fest" that year, a tradition that would carry on for another fifteen years or so. I had my Summer boss to thank for a pool table; even though I hardly had two pennies to rub together, the shared apartment had a relative coziness for having people over, which I enjoyed. The funny thing was that I didn't put much thought into it until I tripped over a weakness that felt like my Achilles' heal.

I had made some new friends from the incoming freshman class at my old dorm and, after hanging out for a while, it seemed so adult to be able to invite them to my place "off campus." After a suitable amount of "we should do it sometimes," we progressed to "Let's have dinner on Friday."

Awesome! My smart and attractive new friends—they were cute girls, if you hadn't guessed—were headed over to hang out with me at "my place." I'm all growed up! Wait a second. Can you hear the record scratch as it dawns on me that I just committed myself to cook dinner for two co-ed beauties, and I don't have a flippin' clue in the kitchen? Now mind you, I learned a couple things as a latchkey kid, the youngest of six. I could make a mean sandwich and was competent at pancakes. In my opinion, I had mastered the omelet, if I had ham and American cheese singles on hand. Not helpful for dinner.

I don't remember exactly how the call went, but pretty soon I was on the phone to Mom. "Mom? How do you make chicken?" As reality dawned that my dinner guests were headed over that day and I was grossly unprepared, I ended up broiling big, unseasoned legs of chicken on a sheet pan. From there my memory goes blank. I think it's my way of protecting myself from the embarrassment.

At that moment, the idea of cooking changed for me. I hadn't given it much thought before; as with most things, I was a self-obsessed, although driven, teenager. Most of the lifestyle maintenance lessons had already gone straight over my head, because I was focused on becoming a rock star or a famous, film-scoring musician.

But amongst these teenage obsessions was also the strong desire to have people over to my place. For the first time, I felt significantly underprepared for the task. I didn't understand the implications, but I knew I didn't want to feel so ill-equipped again. I wanted to learn how to cook.

That Christmas, in response to my panic-riddled call for help, I received a cookbook from my Mom. "The Better Homes and Gardens" one, with the red and white checkered cover. I started slowly; I'd cook one recipe and then repeat it, trying to get comfortable with it, like learning a song. Eventually, within a year or so, I think I cooked through that thing from cover to cover. I'd have to call home for explanations of basic cooking terms, as this story predates the Internet AND Wikipedia. However, the wick was lit—I wanted to cook, and I cherished the opportunity to feed my friends.

This isn't an autobiography, so I'll get on to the beer. Sometime after college, I began homebrewing with my closest college pal. We dug in to the first edition of Charlie Papazian's book, "The Complete Joy of Homebrewing." The idea that we could make beer seemed so underground! We had to drive way out on West Belmont Avenue to the only homebrew supply shop that we knew of in the city of Chicago. We'd hit the buzzer next to the broken screen door and wait for the strange guy to come from the back apartment to let us in. I don't think he ever had our complete list in stock, but he always had a substitute to recommend, and we certainly didn't know enough to question him. His shaking hands would drop the ingredients into a bag, and off we'd go.

I remember discovering the beer industry in 1991, when my friend and homebrewing partner Mike landed a job representing Pilsner Urquell in Chicago for Guinness Import Company. As he described to me how he spent his days encouraging bar owners and shop owners to consider giving more attention to a world-class beer, I was dumbfounded. "That's a job? People do that for a living?"

I was an idealistic music school dropout, hell-bent on refusing to "sell out" to the corporate world of business. I was bar tending and playing gigs; the idea that someone actually managed or encouraged the discussion of beer lists and menus was bewildering to me. Until that moment, in all of my furrowed-brow persistence, I was oblivious to the reality that the principles I held dear in music—artistry, phrasing, and skillful communication of ideas—could be worthwhile in other arenas besides music. I found that not only were they worthwhile, but that my commitment and desire to master them would turn into an invaluable asset for me in the beer industry.

In a few months time, I talked my way into a sales route in downtown Chicago, at one of Mike's distributors, International Brands. We represented hundreds of specialty beers, our biggest being Guinness, Harp, and Bass Ale. While the local Miller distributor owned our division, we were the black sheep of Chicago's busy but narrowly focused beer scene. I took to it like a fish to water and was mesmerized by the landscape in front of me. Chicago is a tough city and a tough market, so I had to learn my lessons fast and well. I had suppliers from all sorts of breweries and importers doing "work-withs," where they'd tag along on my route for a day. As I learned from these suppliers, who were both good and bad, I was immensely drawn to their role of shaping brands, creating opportunities, and championing good beer.

In two short years, I landed a job managing the Midwest for an importer of a German beer, Warsteiner Importers. I was in way over my head, but was willing to work hard to figure it all out. After about a year, I felt I had a handle on the job. I had learned to manage the conversation in many different settings. I could negotiate container-sized orders with the president of a wholesaler one minute, problem-solve with an angry German chef the next, then try to work my beer into a hip rock-club run by a burly, tattooed bar owner.

Micro-brewing started to show up on the scene at this time, and I met one of its pioneers, Larry Bell, at a wholesaler's golf outing. We became fast friends and the hook was set again. My aspirations began to rise as a craft-beer ethos grew inside me like a beer-powered backbone. No longer content to just sell beer, I began to realize that we had an opportunity to change the world. Instead of feeling like I was "selling out" to the game of business, I felt like I had discovered a secret door into it, wherein creative ideas, integrity, and brainstorming were all in abundance, yet a place the rest of the world didn't know about it yet. In 1995, I was hired as the first Sales Manager of Kalamazoo Brewing Company, home of "Bell's Beer."

Things change quickly when your workday includes the smell of multiple mashes in a day. There was a morning in my first week when our specialty brewer, the late Rob Skala, sprang into the shared office at 9:30 am with a hydrometer flask filled with a tank-sample of Java Stout, which he set on my desk. "Let me know what you think," he stated simply, with a grin. I smelled the deep roasty tones of the malted barley. I tasted the chocolate and coffee, edgily dancing each other into a dry, intriguing finish. "It's fucking great."

We faced immense challenges at this point; the company was duct-taped together and rambling down its path with all-but-reckless abandon. No matter the challenges that lay ahead, I knew we could win the battle of flavor. We were making beer that had body, depth, and soul. This was captivating and enthralling, and I was committed to changing the reputation beer had earned from its narrow flavor profiles of the last several decades.

Almost ten years later, in 2004, I left Bell's and joined my friends at New Holland Brewing in Holland, Michigan. I had long appreciated Brett and Jason's approach to brewing, "Art in Fermented Form." The significance of this shift for our galactic flavor travels is that it marks a certain coming of age for me, both in business and in flavor.

I was getting to know new people, new beers and techniques. The experience challenged me to quickly get to know these beers on a personal level in order to express to others what was interesting about them.. I continued to discover my strength of analogy and began to really believe that my palate was my most important tool in learning a beer. Interviewing brewers and remembering ingredients and techniques were important components, but I really began to see the true value of tasting with an open mind.

It was around this time I published my first recipe, Red Tulip Pork Medallions, when All About Beer asked me if we had any recipes for their booklet, "Summer Fare: A Beer Lover's Cookbook." The recipe was later featured in the Detroit Free Press. I had created it from scratch, thinking about the quality of Red Tulip Ale I wanted to accentuate, its unique underlying fruitiness and rich malt character. I thought about function, what you need to make a marinade, and how the beer would be a valuable ingredient.

There were two gratifying moments with that first effort. The Detroit Free Press called to confirm a couple of details, so their test kitchen could try the recipe. Gulp. "It's being tested?" I thought. When they were done and published, their revisions were minor, mostly formatting how ingredients were listed. I thought, "Holy shit, my recipe just survived being tested by a major newspaper. I might just be on to something here." The second gratifying moment was hosting a dinner at my home that included this recipe and our Brewmaster, John. I was confident in my cooking, but did I do the beer proud? My take was that he and the other guests very much enjoyed themselves. What I enjoyed most was hearing them talk about the different flavors they picked up, how things changed, what they noticed or didn't. Whether I could cook or write a recipe wasn't important. I felt I had shared something that helped open the door for people to explore, enjoy, and share flavors with one another.

Seasonal Eating

It is somewhat remarkable that we, as a people, are in need of mentors and teachers to bring us back to eating seasonally. In a couple of decades, our industrialized food industry wiped out generations of habits, tastes, and techniques centered around the natural cycles of seasonal food.

Prior to refrigeration and advances in packaging and shipping that made our food sourcing more global, we focused on foods that were near us and used preservation techniques like curing, smoking, and canning to store food for the off-months. Men, women, and children could tell you what month asparagus grew in and when to expect the family hog to be slaughtered. Harvest time had an impact on everyone, not just the farmers.

I'm no historian, but I can imagine the excitement and congratulations that went around when we learned to vacuum pack, refrigerate, and stabilize foods to keep them from going stale. I imagine a culture coming out of the Great Depression, at war and rationing materials and foods. The idea of a cheap loaf of bread that wouldn't go stale on the shelf, that could be shipped across the country, must have sounded pretty darn useful.

The problem is, we didn't quite realize what we had traded away. What was born from necessity has led to low-priced, nutritionally vacant food and multinational giants that over-engineer food and decimate traditional farming techniques, not to mention financially impacting the farmers themselves.

The most frightening thing is the new norm that was created. We expect one store to carry all foods, from any season, every day. Surprisingly, no one marvels at this feat of magic. The "how" of that trick is not something the normal person even asks about. Check out the produce section next time with a new question: "How in

the world did they manage to get all of these different foods in the same room, at the same time, in this particular town?"

It is a real marvel, and one we benefit from to this day. I have yet to see a lemon, lime, or orange grove in Michigan; if I want citrus, I better hope we know how to ship food. I am willing to bet, though, that the orange I taste from my grocery store probably tasted a little bit better before the two-thousand mile journey. I'd even go so far as to guess that the fruits grown by a small, independent farmer who doesn't grow them by the semi-load might have a slightly different charm to them.

Soapbox aside, there are flavor lessons here. Our palate has thousands of years of hereditary memory; it still remembers the good old days and recognizes foods that grow near each other and harvest at similar times. I can remember sloughing off someone who had some catchy phrase about "what grows together, goes together." But think about it: that was how we once ate. Regardless of whether it's coincidence or Mother Nature, seasonal eating is familiar to our evolved palate. Yanking things from all over the world and opposite ends of the calendar is the confusing part.

What I'm getting at is that the way we eat now is the adaptation, not the other way around. I like to look for opportunities to glean the best of both worlds, expanding my world by being able to taste foods from around the world while holding high standards for what ingredients I'll let into my kitchen.

When you compare this to drinking, our beverages reflect our foods rather than their own harvest cycle. Breweries create beers seasonally but, in most cases, we're using ingredients that have been stored from harvest and held until we want to brew them. There are tasty exceptions but, over time, we have certain flavor profiles at certain times of the year, because our palate, inspired by weather and food patterns, wants them.

I'm surprised at how long it took me to "get it." I was cooking a long time before I actually embraced this ingredient-first mentality. It was another minute before I accepted that I would have to change how I shop to change how I cook and how I eat. Fact is, there are high-level restaurants with chefs who regularly cook and even feature out-of-season ingredients. Some have legitimate sourcing challenges that are met with creative problem solving; others are just oblivious. I'm not saying they're right or wrong; however, I am suggesting that these are sacrifices, conscious or otherwise, and that ingredients will show the distance, some more than others. The closer we can get to the source in time and place, the better.

We're talking about harmony here. Harmony exists when flavors feel right together. Harmony is a natural occurrence that rejects manipulation. Seasonal cooking is not just about eating "local"—it's about looking to nature for lessons and inspiration.

Eating Spring

I can remember, way back in high school, feeling the shift of Spring rolling in. Rolling my window down on that first warm, sunny day changed everything. I can still picture driving up the hill behind my high school, cranking Boston in my '73 Thunderbird with this silly, bright-eyed grin, basking in the sun and fresh air as if I'd never felt it before.

I think that's what I love about Spring: it makes us feel freshness as if it's brand new. Greens look greener, bright seems brighter, and we look forward to each and every fruit or vegetable soon to come our way. That feeling of return and rebirth is what really showcases the beauty of seasonal cooking and eating.

Of course, it's not all rainbows and unicorns. As Prince will tell you, "Sometimes it snows in April," so don't put the wool socks away quite yet, . Instead, prepare to enjoy rootsy, earthy flavors that we like on a rainy day. Spring is a preview season. We start thinking about Summer, but the full-blown glut of fresh foods is still a few months away. Depending on where you are in the world, your fresh selection is still a bit sparse, regardless of your excitement. We count on fresh foods that took us through the Winter—carrots, potatoes, mushrooms, cooking and salad greens—while we welcome broccoli and some cabbages and anxiously await asparagus and rhubarb. We embrace the idea of cooking through our pantry of canned tomatoes, frozen vegetables from Summer, and our pasture-raised meats.

It is a wonderful time for beer, although you'll likely hear that from me in every season. Just as with our foods, we can embrace the hearty flavors we like in cooler weather with porters, stouts, and brown ales—essentially the "comfort food" of the beer world—while we start dosing in flavors that evoke the freshness of the season ahead. I enjoy farmhouse ales like saisons this time of year; their slight sweetness and fruit is countered with nice, subtle spiciness that I love against green veggies. I like soft pales and IPAs for similar reasons. They're outstanding with spicy greens, and their aromas always remind me of herbs, fresh or dried.

Vinaigrette

My concept of vinaigrettes changed forever one evening, somewhere in Northern Italy. My wife Ulla and I were on our honeymoon, enjoying countryside drives, stopping at whatever restaurant looked interesting. As our salads arrived, a spry young server, who couldn't have been a day over seventy, approached us and commandeered the small caddy with bottles of oil and vinegar from our table. In broken English he walked us through the important steps of a basic vinaigrette, gestured at his caddy to express, "this is all you need." He asked for Ulla's fork and spoon and held the spoon over her salad, pouring oil into it while telling us that you shoot for equal parts oil and vinegar. Continuing to hold the spoon out, he set the oil down and picked up the balsamic, pouring it to almost fill the spoon completely. He added a generous pinch of salt and then pepper, although for the life of me I can't remember how he held the spoon AND got ground pepper into it. No matter; he entertained us with his excitement as he led up to the finale. He reached for Ulla's fork and smiled, preparing us for the punch line. He put the tines of the fork into the spoon and stirred it side to side as quickly as possible, careful to only let a little spill over the sides of the spoon. Gradually, he widened his stirring, waxing on the virtues of vinaigrette, intentionally spilling more, moving the spoon across the salad for coverage, and eventually tipping it over to finish. He set the vinaigrette-coated silverware atop the salad, beaming with pride, and said something along the lines of, "That is a vinaigrette." I have never been the same.

His lesson gave me a grasp of what we're trying to accomplish with a vinaigrette, both classic and improvised versions. It's so easy to make as you go, so I feel a little silly giving you recipes, which I don't ever use anymore. Our goal is simple: We want to coat something with a little fat and sweetness (oil), brighten it with acid and tang (vinegar), and season it properly (salt and pepper). You can do this in countless different ways, as long as you're accomplishing the original purpose. You can change the oil if you'd like an accent like sesame, sunflower, or walnut. You can use one of the many vinegars available; I lean towards lighter ones, like rice or white wine vinegar, if I want brightness. Also, beer is acidic, just not as much as wine or vinegar. If I'm building a vinaigrette and want to include beer, I'll typically cut the vinegar by roughly the amount of beer I'm adding, but consider bringing more acid back in via lemon juice or prepared mustard. The mustard has vinegar in it, so it brings in that sharp bite but is going to help adhesion and keep it from getting too wet or loose. If you want sweetness and a little more adhesion, think about natural sweeteners like honey or maple syrup. Soon, you'll understand how "honey mustard" became such a well-known phrase.

While I used the spoon technique for a year or so, I've since moved on, sacrificing the well-appreciated drama for speed and ease. I like to use pint or smaller mason jars with a lid. You can view your build, thinking about one part oil, one part vinegar, for any size batch. Get your ingredients in, shake to emulsify, making sure the vinegar and oil

 spring

have bonded, and taste. You can adjust seasoning, acid, or oil to your palate and re-shake. Feel free to improvise, bringing in other herbs or spices. I enjoy adding Chinese five-spice powder, cardamom and ginger, and other spices for various dishes.

Of course, there are so many places you can take this, but here are three typical builds for beer vinaigrettes. Think about matching intensities between vinegar and beer; if one of them is lighter, the other should follow. I like IPAs for their herbal and aromatic character, lent from the hops. Saisons bring pepper and citrus, while barrel-aged stouts bring a tannic character with earthy roastiness that I love against balsamic and it's buddies.

Vinaigrettes and Salads

Salad greens are full of nutrition and flavor and they fill a great role in terms of balancing our meals. They can bring crispness, brightness, bitterness and spice to your plate depending which greens you choose. You would think these would be hard to find fresh and local in the typical non-harvest seasons, but with greenhouses and hydroponic farming, you'll find you can do pretty well, all year long. In fact, they become a focal point for me through the Winter and early Spring, as they are the brightest, freshest produce going when the snow's on the ground, providing such a nice contrast to the meats, roots and pantry cooking that's getting us through.

With both salad greens and the incoming broccoli and asparagus, simple, clean preparations are best. We've been waiting for these flavors, so we should let them shine through. I enjoy vinaigrettes for this role. They tie things together, providing a little seasoning and acidity, which brightens the flavors on our palate. Doesn't that sound like we just described a saison? So whether you use a vinaigrette or not, we can build on our palate memory, which says, "I like these things together." Remember to look for slight acidity, peppery notes, and brightness when pairing to fresh Spring vegetables. For instance, I know asparagus is delightful in a light vinaigrette. But, more often than not I'm grilling it or sautéing it with nothing more than a little oil, salt, and pepper. Since, I know what it likes, I can borrow the ideas from a mild vinaigrette that typically use citrus, spice, and acid and head towards saisons, pales, IPAs, and even mild sours that showcase similar flavors.

IPA Vinaigrette

makes 1/4 cup

1 tablespoon extra virgin olive oil

2 tablespoon rice vinegar

1 tablespoon honey

1 tablespoon IPA

1 tablespoon lemon juice

1/2 teaspoon kosher salt

1/2 teaspoon black pepper

Monkey King Vinaigrette

makes 1/3 cup

2 tablespoon extra virgin olive oil

1 tablespoon rice vinegar

1 tablespoon maple syrup

1 tablespoon stone-ground mustard

2 tablespoon saison

1 teaspoon kosher salt

1/2 teaspoon black pepper

Dragon's Milk Vinaigrette

makes 1/4 cup

2 tablespoon extra virgin olive oil 2 tablespoon balsamic vinegar

1 tablespoon Dragon's Milk (bourbon barrel stout)

3 drops truffle oil

1 teaspoon kosher salt

1 teaspoon black pepper

Asparagus Chevre Salad

Serves 4-6

Asparagus is a poster child for seasonal eating. When it is in season, it is robust, plentiful, and delicious. This pleasant salad plays on its brightness and puts forward fresh, clean flavors of Spring. Delightful with saisons and pale ales.

20 asparagus spears, trimmed and sliced on a bias into 1 inch bites

Salt and pepper, to taste

6-8 radishes, cleaned and thinly sliced

1/2 lb. fresh chevre (goat cheese)

Extra virgin olive oil

Juice of 1/4 lemon

Toss asparagus lightly in oil and season with salt and pepper. Sauté or grill in basket 5-8 minutes until bright green, yet still toothsome. Remove to bowl and add radishes, lemon juice, and a little additional olive oil. Toss before adding goat cheese by the spoonful, and lightly toss to finish and serve.

Alternately, blanch asparagus, strain, toss with radishes and Monkey King Vinaigrette, add chevre and lightly toss to finish and serve.

The Art of Pairing

The Palate

Somewhere along the line, I began to think of my palate as a living thing. I realized it had memory, preferences, and sensitivities. Hell, it even had a job! It started as a joke, but as I gave it more room to breathe, the idea and my palate came alive.

Think about the thoughts, messages, and details you process after tasting something. Whenever you taste something, your mind and palate come alive with conversation. Did you like it? Have you had it before? Does it remind you of something else? Is it sweet? Bitter? Something you can't quite figure out? What are the things you LOVE to taste, and what do you hate? Ever thought about why, or wondered who made the decision?

For years, I did not like blue cheese. My palate and I accepted that as fact without discussing it. We simply knew that my palate was the doorman, and blue cheese was on the do-not-admit list. I wasn't grossed out or repulsed by it, but I knew I didn't care for it. With my palate and nose cooperating, I would know if blue cheese was on the plate before the server arrived at the table, and I would carefully remove it.

One night, eating at the bar at a local tapas joint, Fandango, I had a bite of blue cheese from a mixed platter. Much to my surprise, it tasted pretty good. I tried another bite—delicious. I asked the bartender about it, writing down the name and origin to save for later. I had found the one blue cheese I enjoyed, and I looked forward to finding it again and repeating the experience.

The following week, I ate five or six different blue cheeses. From careful little bits to spoonfuls of chunky, smelly, mold-ripened glory, I ate it all; I was on a blue cheese bender.

What changed?

My tongue didn't have some physical transformation. The cheese was there all along, in all of it's blue-ness. At the tapas bar I enjoyed a blue cheese, and my palate—the doorman to my gut—took it off the list. This established a theory of mine I call "Palate Alarms."

I believe the palate's original job was to keep us alive by rejecting things that would poison us. Poisonous plants taste bad. Rancid meat smells and tastes awful. Our palate has assigned those emotional words to these bad things, so we stay well away. The thing is, sometimes it is over-protective, or worse yet, melodramatic. Remember that food you got sick on as a kid? Your palate sure does. I'll bet, if you think about it for a minute, you'll swear you can taste it right now. The liquor you won't drink because of that "one time?" Think about it... There it is; you can imagine the sensation of its flavor and aroma and, in this case, it's attached to some traumatic tasting experience.

Our palate has a memory and a responsibility to keep us from consuming bad things in the first place, and it certainly doesn't want us repeating "mistakes." Now, I wouldn't bring these tasting traumas up just to torment you; I point to them as signs of life. If our palate is making these discretionary judgments, I argue that perhaps a more meaningful dialogue is available.

I have seen many people at beer tastings with palate alarms on and in effect. Bitterness is the most common culprit, followed by anything dark. My role as Beervangelist in these situations takes one of two directions. Either I negotiate with the palate about accepting this scofflaw flavor, or I adeptly steer the drinker to other flavors their palate deems acceptable.

Now, I wouldn't blame you for thinking, "What does this have to do with anything?" However, stay with me for a minute and I'll share how productive this concept can be.

We're going to leave the alarms alone for now and dig back into the idea of your palate having a memory. This comes in very handy when we try to describe anything we taste. Beer profiles are filled with descriptors, words that are actually related to other things. If nothing ever tasted "like" anything else, each flavor would have its own word, and we'd have a very hard time ordering from a menu. I can tell you that a beer is nutty or has flavors of caramel, chocolate, or coffee, creating an expectation that will be delivered on.

The idea of "an acquired taste" always intrigued me. Apparently, there's a difference between things we like innately and things we teach ourselves to like, get used to, or maybe just learn as an adult. So, what is it that drives the shift?

One theory I've heard states that we start out as babies with very sensitive palates, which slowly become less sensitive. This explains why we don't see babies eating blue cheese and drinking scotch. As we grow older, we cannot only handle more aggressive flavors, but we seek them out in order to experience the intensity of flavor we're used to. This explains a few things about the elderly and salt.

Another theory I'd like to offer is that the strained-peas-and-mashed-carrots era of our life doesn't establish a baseline for certain flavors that adults love but kids hate. Things like olives, blue cheese, coffee, beer, and whiskey start out as very foreign flavors to our palate; thus, they are often treated as outsiders without credentials. The palate alarm goes off when intruders are detected, and it sends a message to the brain that induces scrunched nose, closed eyes, pursed lips, and maybe a head shake or two.

I believe that most times, you're one or two positive experiences away from turning off the alarm and adding to your list of favorite things. When did you start liking coffee? Was it the first sip? Or, when you imagine that moment you first liked it, do you imagine cupping your hands around a warm mug on a Saturday morning while you sat in your pjs and dawdled over a crossword puzzle? Or sitting by a fire on a memorable camping trip? Your series of moments, especially enjoyable ones, inform your sense of adventure.

That's all well and good, but how do we use this strange theory? Pairing well creates lots of positive flavor memories. It links flavors together harmoniously, often accentuating our favorite parts, or even bringing sec-

ondary flavors out that we may not have tasted before. For one thing, I think this is an act of kindness; hearing "I've had this plenty of times, but it's never tasted like that before" from your palate is a sign you've kept it interested and engaged rather than bored.

Secondly, pairing can turn alarms off. When one of your palate alarms is breached successfully, it doesn't seem quite as scary. People with sensitivities or who just don't like hops, dark beers, or stinky cheese, for instance, may enjoy them when they're paired well. This means beer dinners are the most important place to keep an open mind and try everything. Who knows, that one positive experience may just get a flavor in the door and straight to the VIP room.

Flavor First

I often find myself describing the benefits of my flavor-first philosophy as a way to explain beer to new or non- beer drinkers. If I use technical terms when describing beer or food, it's more likely the person I'm speaking to, and their palate, have no idea what I'm talking about. If you describe a taste as hoppy to someone who has never had hops before, you may as well be speaking Greek, as they say, especially since it's not an ingredient we grow up around. If we talk about the flavors that hops remind us of and reference thoughts, flavors, and memories people's palates have experienced before, then our language becomes universal—and much more useful.

The newborn beer palate is a very illustrative example, but this idea is certainly not limited to beginners. Quite the contrary. I feel that operating from a flavor-first perspective has improved my tasting experience and made me more open-minded and versatile when it comes to pairing.

Flavor first is a simple concept: it's just an adjustment to how people have been taught to understand beer in the past. We used to start every server training or Beer 101 class by explaining that all beers were either a lager or an ale. We would then point to Michael Jackson's well-organized genealogical beer tree and show how all styles were descendants of one side or the other. Furthermore, the explanation would continue by establishing that whether the beer is an ale or a lager depends on which family of yeast was used in its production and whether it was top fermented or bottom fermented. Imagining any flavors, yet? Me neither.

Not surprisingly, this method doesn't conjure up flavor memories, nor does it help people find their next beer. For instance, I can't tell you how many thousands of guests have come up to a tasting table I'm working, held their glass out in front of me, and said, "I'll have the ale." One problem, of course, is that more often than not, the table is full of ales, just different styles. So at the risk of making them feel bad for not ordering well, I have to get more information if I'm going to help them choose something they'll like. Secondly, their request didn't give me any head start, as "ale" has very little bearing on primary flavors. The world of ales includes the whole gamut of beer flavors, so I don't know any more about their preferences for sweet, bitter, dark, light, big, or small. I have no indication of what flavors will be more pleasing for them than others. That all-important first chapter of beer organization into ales and lagers fails miserably when not surrounded by other context.

As I got deeper into pairing, I realized the theme continued. The chef, a flavor ambassador, didn't need to know about which way the yeast fermented; he needed to know what flavors were present and which lay beneath as secondary flavors that might be coaxed forward with a creative pairing. Even in an advanced setting, our style tree was proving purposeless.

At some point, I decided I wanted to throw out whatever materials I had been using or had written. I thought about what my first questions to myself were when selecting a beer, either for myself or for a pairing. What were the broader categories that divided drinkers and their preferences or alarms? Clearly, malt and hops are the first two. But if I go back to my newborn palate consideration, I'm going to have to explain both of those words with something better than "malty" and "hoppy." In order to think of beers this way, we'll have to really think about universal flavor words even before we think about which beers or beer styles we want there.

If we learn to talk in flavors, we also learn to listen to them. When I'm tasting beer or food, I like to quiet my brain and listen to my palate. Style is irrelevant when I'm getting to know a beer. The aroma and taste develop throughout several sips, from the first sniff and taste to that subtle character that lingers long after the swallow. Each sip may taste different as I acclimate to it, as it warms... All these inputs help me get to know a beer a little better.

This creates a memory that I can draw upon later. I was recently asked if I liked to take notes to recall beers or styles for the purpose of pairing, and I was amused by my answer. I explained that I really preferred to conjure up flavors and draw upon my palate's memory. If I'm tasting a food and considering what I want to drink with it, I imagine flavors first. Do I want roast? Caramel? Citrus? I can feel my palate trying these flavors on for size. My senses recollect previous experiences more effectively than words. While imagining these characteristics, I'm able to feel whether or not they fit the circumstance. All before I've taken a sip or mentioned a style.

By grouping flavors into four families, I get a broad range of likely cohorts from various styles. Once you're in a compatible family of flavors, it's likely you'll have several choices that can be pleasing—whether you're pairing to a person or a plate. For instance, if I find that somebody likes the rich, roasty flavors of malt, it's likely I can bring them several beers from that family, all of various styles, that will be similarly pleasing.

From there, I can tailor the experience with subtler nuances between specific styles or producers. These smaller details are really "finish work," however, as the pairing itself was based upon the broader stroke of thinking about flavor families.

While we're flavor first with our palate, our brain likes to organize things it can access later. Here's where styles and brands really come into play. I like to use them as a card catalogue of sorts, an index where I can go to find beers that I know have the flavors that will satisfy my request. They'll lead you to the territory of not one but several viable choices, which makes it easier to repeat pleasant experiences.

Flavors of Beer

Malt-Forward Flavors

When I think of the flavors that abound in malt-forward beers, I think of a wide range of flavors: biscuits and bread, caramel, roastiness, toastiness, and even nuttiness. There's also a secondary, fruit-like sweetness at times: apricots, pears, or peaches. I imagine darker flavors like molasses, toffee, coffee, and chocolate. Of course, they're not necessarily all present at one time but, to me, these flavors have a lot of commonality. We could get into how that came to be, but let's remember that our palate is not planning to brew at the moment—it's planning to taste.

This common overlap, however, will be very useful. These flavors often play well together, both in how we eat and drink. We can use that familiarity to both determine whether we like something and to make a pretty good guess at what it might go with.

Descriptors: Roasty, sweet, caramel, stone fruit, toasty/toasted, coffee, chocolate, corn

Malt-Forward Styles: Where to find these flavors:

Ales

- Amber
- Brown/Scotch/ESB
- Porter
- Stout
- Barleywine/Wheatwine

Lagers

- Bock/Dopplebock
- Amber Lager
- Marzen/Oktoberfest
- Dortmund
- Helles

Hop-centric Flavors

On to hops. I suppose I should stop being surprised at how many people use this word as if the entire universe were hip to it. We're far enough along in this beer renaissance that I imagine the percentage of people that understand what we mean by "hoppy" is growing, but that really misses the point. What flavors are present when we showcase hops? They are very aromatic, with citrus, grassy, and herbal characteristics. Citrus is often grapefruit-like, or maybe like orange and lemon. Bright bitterness is in this family of flavors, as well as acidity and evergreen or pine-like flavors. Again, they're not all present all the time, but you can see similarities and how they play together.

Descriptors: Grassy, floral, grapefruit (citrus), pine, aromatic, bitter, herbal, acidic, cleansing

Hop-centric Styles: Where to find these flavors:

Ales

- Pale Ale
- India Pale Ale (IPA)
- Double/Imperial IPAs

Lagers

- Pilsner

From the Cellar: The Flavor of Fermentation

This category is the Grand Canyon between most brains and palates. If you're not a brewer, baker, or cheesemaker, hearing a beer has a very pronounced fermentation character doesn't help you much. The fact is, our palates are familiar with these flavors; we're just not used to having them described by their origin or technique.

Even now, writing this, I have to resist the urge to start my explanation with how they are created. We'll get to it, because I think it will help you understand the context and feel, but we must remember our flavor-first concept and start with what they taste like.

Beers in this family present a range of flavors from fruits like banana, green apple, apricot, and plum as well as citrus. They can also include spiciness that may present as clove, black pepper or, in more rare instances, cinnamon. Tartness or sourness is also part of this family and can be a mild, supporting role or the primary characteristic. I also associate a mineral-like character to this family. I think of beers with complex earthiness that reminds me of mineral water or sauvignon blanc as belonging to this family as well.

Since the process, "fermentation," is the name of the flavor family, it seems reasonable to provide a little explanation. It's different from most of the others because it is a process rather than an ingredient you can hold or smell. Granted, the ingredient that starts it all is yeast, but the process of fermentation that it kicks off is really where the flavor is. While all beers are fermented, not all showcase the esters or flavor compounds that are born

from the process.

Other food and drink showcase similar flavors, such as sourdough bread, yogurt, and kombucha tea. That tangy tartness or background spice profile that can be present in these treats bears remarkable similarity to flavors found in these beers, but people don't often identify them by their process, fermentation. To make matters more confusing, words like "sour" often make people brace for something terrible. From our palate's point of view, this makes sense. Wine left on the counter too long starts to sour, and that's bad; your palate, along with your nose, tells you to stay away. Vinegar, on the other hand, is aged intentionally, taking enough of a bad thing and turning it good again. Cheese is the same way. Furry cheese abandoned in your fridge? Not so good. Stinky blue cheese with veins of funk from bacteria gone wild? Delicious.

I find that identifying the flavors before the process helps us talk to our palate more plainly. "Tart" sets up "sour" and "acidic" because tart has positive connotations that create the expectation of sourness and acidity, so they're not such a surprise.

Descriptors: Clean, crisp, fruity, apple, pear, peach, banana, plum, tart, sour, tangy, spicy, pepper, clove

Cellar-forward Styles: Where to find these flavors:

Ales

- Wheat
- White
- Hefeweizen
- Saison
- Farmhouse
- Belgian (double, triple)
- Lambic and other fruit beers

Wood-aged and Fruit: Freestyle!

This family of flavors is the catch-all, freestyle family. I focus on wood aging and fruit in the title, as those are very common examples. Essentially, this is the category that holds the flavors born from ingredients or processes outside of the typical beer experience. So if a brewer, by way of their label, has told us they're bringing in new ingredients such as fruit, barrels, coffee, or chocolate, we can taste for the subsequent flavors.

Let's start with barrel aging. Flavors can come from the wood as well as the spirit that may have been previously aged in the barrel, such as bourbon, sherry, or rum. What does wood taste like? I'm glad you asked, because that's what our palate needs to know.

Wood-aged beers tend to include various notes of vanilla or coconut. You may pick up specific woody notes, or oakiness, but we don't always have words for this. After all, we're not accustomed to sucking on oak chips. The vanilla and oakiness from the vanillin and toasted char of the barrel have delicious relevance to our taste buds.

Fruit will, of course, bring whatever flavor it's known for; raspberry and cherry are frequently chosen as tasty additions. Besides their overt flavors, they can also bring a brightness, maybe some tartness, and even the perception of effervescence. I find raspberries in particular to liven a beer's feel on my tongue, the sensation known as mouthfeel. The bright, punctuated notes and lively tingliness on my palate make me think of sparkling wine or bubbly water. This may or may not be reflected with actual carbonation, but think about how your mouth reacts to fresh raspberries and you know it's part of its overall characteristic that wakes your palate up.

Coffee beers are another fun example in this family. Of course, as we've seen in the malt-forward family, you don't need to have coffee to have coffee flavor, but you certainly can. These beers bring overt coffee roast to the game, increased acidity, and edgy bitterness.

The same goes for chocolate, a flavor often associated with malted barley and, thus, malty beers. We can also introduce chocolate or cacao nibs as an ingredient, thus intensifying the flavor experience and bringing in oils and flavors that shape how we taste and feel the beer.

Descriptors: Oakiness (or wood), vanilla, coconut, spirit (bourbon, wine, sherry, rum, etc.), fruit, tartness, sweetness, fruit of choice (raspberry, cherry, etc.)

Wood-aged or Freestyle Beers: Where to find these flavors:

Typically an identified, "add-on" style

• Barrel-Aged _____ "

• "Ale brewed with _____ "

Lambic

Expectation of Change: The Art of Pairing

I've mentioned a few times that I use the same tools and concepts to pair to people's palates as I do to pair food. There is a shift that happens, however, when we start talking about the art of beer and food pairings. Pairing is the act of bringing two things together with the expectation of change, but it goes beyond eating and drinking together. I often remind people that eating something nice next to something nice to drink is not a bad way to spend an evening, but it's not necessarily pairing.

Pairing, whether intentional or not, is when the beer and the food excite something in each other. They can harmonize and accentuate signature flavors, or they can contrast with each other in dynamic and pleasing counterpoint. Sometimes the beer changes your perception of the food; other times, it's the other way around. Directing the change is something of a skill, but it all starts with recognizing that you are looking for an exchange of energy or flavor between the two.

I'd like to bring us back to the idea of mindfulness for a moment. The important idea here is to take a moment to consider what exchange you'd like between your food and drink. Or, perhaps just listen to whatever conversation the two have already started.

Pairings do not have to be complicated. They do not require extra work—you'll lift your glass and fork just the same as before. It's really about relaxing and taking in the tastes and sensations that live between the two things.

There are times when the interaction may show up as a surprise, when you notice a shift as you are having a casual meal. Other times, it's as simple as ordering or making what you like and knowing that the shape of the meal includes your drink.

My wife Ulla is not much of a beer drinker, but she grew up in Denmark. In that country there are certain meals like rugbrød—a collection of various veggies and meats on dark pumpernickel bread with either mayo or remoulade and crunchy onions—that require a cold lager. It's not a light suggestion of "maybe we should have a beer"; without one, she might reconsider the meal. It's also not a complex experience where she needs a Sommelier or Cicerone to select a rare, exotic beer. Her palate simply says at the outset, "These flavors go together—I'd like a clean, bright, slightly sweet, yet bready beer with this food." In other words, a light, European-style lager or, in a pinch, a crisp kölsch or blonde ale is required.

My point is that the experience is as simple, complex, luxurious, or comfy as you choose to make it. It can be a recurring favorite or a bold new adventure. You can follow guidelines, like many that I'll share with you throughout this book, or you can just follow your gut. There are typical compositions that make sense to our palates. We know certain things "go together," and often the best pairings play off some of those memorable, cultural examples or "Greatest Hits." Chocolate goes with vanilla, and nuts are nice with caramel. These give us

Describe Flavors to Communicate, Not to Impress

Whether we're telling a friend about something we think they'd like or writing tasting notes, the goal is really the same. We're conveying ideas about flavor, trying to get another human being to understand the experience we're having with our palate. Seems simple enough, right?

These days, whether in casual conversation or as part of our new digital habit of blogging and reviewing just about anything, I feel that we sometimes lose our way.

I love that people are talking about beer, tasting critically, and expressing themselves. My problem is that it seems people are inclined to write critically, forming an immediate opinion with the goal of judging a beer's worth for others. There seems to be an emphasis on quantity and tallying up reviews like notches on a bedpost. I also notice a trend to choose impressive descriptors over more expressive ones.

I encourage people to take inspiration from great writers and speakers. Who do we like to read or listen to? Is it the people with fancy words, or those who tell us what we should like? Not for me. I want to hear from someone who is using vocabulary and phrasing to express ideas or experiences. To me, great speakers are the ones who get their points across. They are eloquent, draw you in, create interest and suspense as you look forward to each sentence or new idea. Take me there. Tell me what it was like.

If you're the only one who's ever tasted or imagined tasting the descriptive word you want to use, it's useless to anyone else. To have purpose, descriptors must have familiarity; they must be common enough to conjure up thoughts, yet unique enough to describe momentary detail. You want people to be able to imagine the flavor as you describe it. To me, an overly abstract description reads as egotistical judgment. "Clearly you would taste the nutshell and chalk if you were as accomplished a taster as I..."

A good novelist describing a wooded path might describe the color of the leaves or the way the light shined through the trees, perhaps the smell of yesterday's rain. As a reader and a human, I am completely capable of deciding whether I like the sound of that path or not—so the writer doesn't need to tell me how to feel about it. She just needs to get me to imagine the path as if I were there.

Whitefish
Rack of Lamb
Grilled Asparagus
Salad w/IPA Vin.
Crepe Duxelle
Lamb Stew

examples to riff on and an understanding of our tendencies, but there are no rules. We all have our own sensitivities, so what I find absolutely wonderful may not be right for you.

So, while I'll champion your right to drink as you please, I'll also challenge you to keep an open mind when it comes to pairing. When you mindfully and artfully combine flavors, they often create an experience that is more subtle or composed than the two things separately.

I've seen it hundreds of times: big, assertive beers, paired with harmonious foods, act light on their feet. Their intense flavors are somehow more "in place" when combined with the right food components. People who are sure they don't like stouts taste them against chocolate and reconsider everything they thought they knew about the beer. I've heard phrases like, "I don't normally like hops, but with this dish, this beer was delicious" more times than I can count.

Oftentimes, a positive experience like this may turn off the alarm you've had with a particular style or flavor. Other times, it may mean you find the flavor too assertive or outside of your comfort zone unless it's with something compatible. If so, you can plan your future experiences accordingly.

In short, you'll find that guidelines take you to certain places and pairings that are pleasing for most people. When you're at a hosted event with experts putting together the pairings, you might find some increase in adventure or some surprising new twists. All of this feeds your palate memory and informs your own sense of what you'd like to repeat, tweak, or maybe even what isn't right for you. I do think you'll find that including your drink as part of your overall composition, whether it's a fancy dinner or a Tuesday night at home, will provide pleasure, harmony, and flavor that makes any food-and-drink experience all that much more enjoyable.

Flavor Bridges

Pairing well really hinges on connecting, or bridging, flavors together. To me, there's the overall experience of tasting something, but within that, there are key flavors that stand out. These flavors stand out because they're either the most significant or familiar to your palate; other times, flavors may stand out because they play well with others.

This is part of tasting and pairing that may get a little more detailed then just determining whether you like something or not. It's not necessarily any more technical, just more detailed. As you finish tasting something, you really need to set aside some of your normal processing and just ask yourself "what's here... what is that like?"

You've already noticed that I talk in flavor bridges quite a bit. I've pointed out caramel notes, grapefruit, coffee, or chocolate. Recognize that in these examples, the flavor can be prominent or subtle but, either way, it is part of the supporting cast for the entire experience. It does not necessarily imply a dominating flavor; rather, it means you can have hints of coffee without having a coffee-flavored beer.

When we take the step to pairing, these flavor bridges are what influence our choices. We can decide we want to bring the flavor further forward, accentuating it by focusing attention on it. We can also bridge to "known companions," setting these flavors against things they go with when they're not part of a beer description.

Think about all of the flavor descriptors we've used already and realize they're all descriptions of other things we like to taste and like to taste by themselves as well as with other things. Without even knowing it, we're already experienced at pairing flavors found in beer.

We know darker, roasty flavors like chocolate and coffee do well against creamy dairy and vanilla without knowing anything about beer. We serve cream with coffee, chocolate cake with vanilla ice cream, and so on. It makes perfect sense, then, to juxtapose those flavors, simply changing the context. Perhaps the coffee is from a stout and the cream is represented by a soft-ripened brie, or even a vanilla-laced flan or custard desert. That fresh squeeze of lemon you serve with fish? It's a great cue to think about a beer with some bright citrus tones. These relationships aren't new to our palate; we've just presented them in a fresh context. By opening your mind to the various components of both your food and your beer, you can see natural partners and lead yourself to otherwise counterintuitive pairings.

I like to keep my palate entertained so it enjoys going to work. One of the ways I like to do this is by accentuating secondary flavors, bringing a spotlight to the supporting cast members that may have not been noticed but were there all along. I find these pairings to bring intrigue and interest, maybe even suspense. I enjoy it when I feel like my palate is saying, "Wow—I've had that a million times, but it never tasted like THAT before." The way to do this is, of course, to recognize the flavor bridges you want to accentuate in the first place. There are a number of ways to accomplish this recognition, but the process starts by understanding and sensing the various flavors available and then artfully bridging to one or more.

This brings us to another important point. You can't pair to, match, or otherwise activate all of the flavors available all of the time. I implore you to not waste your time trying. I often joke that one of the benefits of beer and food is that nothing can really go all that wrong. Well, there are a few exceptions; most of the ones I've experienced have come from over-engineering, trying too hard to get to it all and losing my palate along the way.

Whether it's a single course or a full dinner plate of a few items, the concept is the same. Pick out a couple of key flavors as your bridges and think about what you'd like next to them. "Key" is whatever you decide it is, and it will likely benefit from the moment you start thinking about it.

The components of the dish are already a composition. Whether you made it or not, somebody decided the sauce, meat, and starch—or whatever—go well together. So you can throw a line to whichever flavor in whichever component speaks to you. By successfully pairing to one, you will be hooked up and connected to the others.

Sometimes I imagine throwing a line to a cleat on a pier. I only need that one connection and I can gently glide the whole boat to rest. My other abstract analogy is the second instance of the "Doorman Theory." Once you're successfully bridged to one element, you're "in," as they already get along with the others and are happy to vouch for you throughout the plate.

Remember that this is only as complex as you make it. By thinking of simple, memorable flavors, you're able to activate the more confident and instinctual part of your palate memory. Think about what the flavors remind you of and what you'd like with them. It's really that simple.

Match Intensity

Perhaps the simplest of pairing guidelines is also the most present in all pairings, and that's the idea of matching intensity. Simply put, you want to have similar degrees of intensity in your food and your beverage. Intensities don't have to be the same character or flavor, and they don't need to be exactly the same level of assertiveness. If they get too far out of balance, though, one or the other will fade away and yield to the bigger of the two.

This isn't necessarily unpleasant, it just misses some of the potential of a good or great pairing. When you're working with a flavor-first perspective, it's also the easiest to address. If the beer's too big and dominates the food, just think about the flavors you chose the beer for in the first place, and ask whether there are other brands or styles that keep the flavor but dial back the intensity. For instance, if a barleywine is running over a dessert, how about keeping caramel present with an old ale, dopplebock, or amber ale?

Of course, the opposite holds true as well. If the food is more intense than the beer, use the moment to check with your palate; maybe you like the flavor bridges, but just need more intensity. If so, look to neighboring brands or styles to find a good fit without really overhauling your intentions about the pairing. You're just using your brand and style "index" to dial in the fit.

Oftentimes, these are "next time" fixes. It's pretty rare that I run into a miss with intensity where it's actually unpleasant. It's more a memory note my palate and I make together to store for next time. If you're in a relaxed setting, it's also a good time to try a couple similar beers with varying intensities side by side and talk about which one really hits the mark.

Matching intensity is a general guideline that will improve your selections and create balance in your pairings. It's a subjective call, one of those things you'll need to taste for yourself, as the intensity of traditional beers or foods really varies among chefs, cooks, and brewers. Luckily, eating and drinking to inform our palate is hardly an arduous task.

Four C's of Pairing

I can't remember when I first wrote down the Four Cs of Pairing. I'm pretty sure I was paraphrasing and improvising on some points made by one of my early mentors, Lucy Saunders. I often gave beer and food presentations for salespeople and servers, and I was looking for ways to simplify my explanation of the role played by pairing. I felt breaking it down into simple actions would help people understand what we were trying to accomplish and the similarities across many pairings.

After years of including the Four Cs they became an even stronger part of my pairing philosophy. Interestingly enough, though, their "place" in my method went through a bit of a reversal.

In the beginning, I used them as a pairing tip: "In order to pair, you will choose one of these." After many presentations and hundreds of conversations, I came to realize that the way I explained pairing was not very true to how I actually went about it. Though true in some sense, the statement pushes toward an almost academic posture when thinking of flavor companions, rather then the instinctive, intuitive palate memory that I'm so fond of counting on.

The importance of the Four C's didn't fade; I just realized they served a slightly different purpose. Remember the idea that the art of pairing includes the expectation of change? Well, in order for change to be perceived as positive, it really needs to serve a purpose or fulfill a role in some way. The Four Cs are really four essential roles that define enjoyable change through pairing.

Let's take a look at each one of them and see what I mean.

Complement: Combining similar flavors to accentuate or amplify through their unity or harmony. A nutty amber ale brings forward the nuttiness of a gruyere, perhaps in a way you never noticed before the two were together. Dark chocolate bridges to the dark, chocolaty flavors in a roasty stout, immersing the diner in a cozy blanket of chocolate bliss. Complementing flavors are often part of drawing secondary flavors forward.

Contrast: Flavors that are not like one another in pleasant counterpoint. Bright, floral IPAs contrast against sharp cheddar, just as roasty stout does against a soft-ripened double-crème cheese. Contrasting flavors are some of our strongest flavor memories.

Cleanse: No matter how enjoyable the flavor experience, there are times where we need to whisk our palate clean to provide a refreshing break between bites or sips. Assertive flavors can linger and cloud our ability to taste. Whether it's spicy heat or rich fatty foods, a cleansing pairing will punctuate a bold flavor experience, putting a period on the sentence and creating a fresh second bite. Bitterness and acidity are frequent go-tos for this role. Hops bring overt bitterness that is a nice cleanse against spice, as is the edgy, roasted bitterness of dark stouts. Tart, acidic sour ales are a bright, cleansing sip against rich pâtés or roasted duck.

Sauteed Whitefish with Sautéed Spinach Salad

As we head towards the brighter flavors of Spring, it's a wonderful time to enjoy fish. Growing up in the upper Midwest, after many years of oblivion, I've been counseled by my chef friends that if it doesn't swim in a sea, it ain't seafood. This of course, was news to me, as I referred to every fish as seafood. Regardless, in our neck of the woods we have the magnificent Great Lakes and their freshwater fish. Available anytime, I find the tender, delicate flavor of whitefish and perch to play nicely with the food and beer of Spring. They're slightly sweet, take lighter acids well, like lemon or vinaigrette, and bring brightness to our plates as we look forward to the days getting longer. This spinach salad and sautéed whitefish is fairly simple and a delightful pair to saisons. Swap in some arugula for the spinach and either change up your vinaigrette or make an herbed aioli and you have a whitefish plate or sandwich built for easygoing pale ales.

Serves 6-8

Spinach Salad

2-3 shallots, minced

Olive oil

Salt and pepper, to taste

3/4-cup carrots, julienned

5 cloves of garlic, minced

4 cups spinach, chopped

Sweat shallots and carrots in oil 3-5 minutes or until tender. Add garlic, top with spinach almost immediately, and season with salt and pepper. Continue 3 minutes or so until tender, toss in vinaigrette, and remove to plate.

Vinaigrette:

1/4-cup olive oil

1/8-cup saison

1/8-cup white balsamic vinegar

Juice from 1/2 lemon

1 teaspoon horseradish

1 teaspoon salt

1 teaspoon pepper

Combine ingredients, shake or stir aggressively until emulsified.

Whitefish Fillets:

2 whitefish fillets

2 teaspoon salt/2 teaspoon pepper

1/2 cup flour

1/2 lemon

Season fish with a pinch of salt and pepper. Stir flour and remaining salt and pepper together. Dust whitefish in seasoned flour. Sauté whitefish in oil over medium heat, roughly 3 minutes per side. Set fillets on top of salad, top with a squeeze of lemon and serve with your favorite saison.

Create: There are times when sips and bites come together and something else altogether happens. There are flavors that result from combinations that seem to evolve from nowhere and everywhere and aren't experienced unless and until these things combine. This is the most rare of the Cs, but definitely a galactic experience. My first was a big hunk of Maytag blue cheese with sips of Dragon's Milk washing over it. If I could describe it, I would.

So, the idea here is that each of the Four Cs describes some positive change from the two items being put together or paired. To that end, a good pairing should have at least one C. This means it has purpose to our palate and positive change in mind. It may have more than one; in fact, it's possible (but not necessary) to have all four! As I've worked with these, I find it important to be able to look at them from both directions. There are times to use them in creating the pairing, recognizing a bridge. Thinking, "Oh... I'd like to complement that" is perfectly natural. However, it's also nice to apply the Four Cs in reverse. After intuitively selecting a pair, and while experiencing it, just think "What's happening here?" If none of the Cs are happening, you're just eating and drinking, and I suppose there are worse things than that.

Organizing your memories by thinking about which C or Cs took place will help you express the idea to others and/or recreate similar experiences in the future

Drinking Spring

Malt: Reds, Ambers, and Bocks

Amber ales were once the hallmark of craft brewers, their signature in flavor. Their reddish brown hue and deep malty flavors set them apart from the golden, light lagers that dominated the mainstream. Caramel tones from malted barley are the stars of the show in this style, leading our palates in a dance between toasted notes and rich sweetness.

Our palate recognizes and appreciates these flavors because they are prominent throughout many of our favorite foods. The tasty brown crust of freshly baked bread, the crispy skin of roasted poultry, the sweet and nutty flavor of sautéed onions, and the roasted character of the malted barley of amber ales all share similarities in flavor due to a chemical reaction called the Maillard reaction, often mislabeled with the sugar term caramelization.

Whatever you call the reaction, we like to eat things that have been browned with heat. From memory, we can conjure up the difference between lightly toasted biscuits, the deep brown crust of a soft pretzel, and the dark grill marks on a juicy steak. These flavorful examples illustrate how well these flavors play with others. They are complementary flavor bridges that thrive in combination with similar flavors.

Take for instance a grilled burger with sautéed onions on a toasted bun. Each one of those ingredients accentuates the similarities of the other, bridging the roasty, toasty, slightly sweet, browning/Maillard characteristics. It's that immediate harmonization that makes amber ales such a natural with not only this imagined burger, but with food in general. The tasty characteristics demonstrated in ambers are a big reason why beer is such as a wonderfully agile beverage when it comes to food pairings. Beer shares this flavor bridge with food more than any other beverage in the world.

Brewers have plenty of room to interpret within this somewhat wide style, but I find the caramel tones and slight nuttiness to be the most common trait. You'll find similar characteristics in neighboring styles such as amber lager, alt, and even red ales. Expect hops to provide supporting secondary flavors unless otherwise specified, such as in "hoppy amber."

Today it seems these styles are sometimes overlooked, as IPAs became more brewers' hallmarks and beer fans regale other dynamic and exciting styles craft brewers are known for. We would be well served to keep amber ales in our sights, on our menus, and in our fridges, as they are quintessential "food beers." They are the utility-infielders or "Manny Trillos" of food pairings, as they can bridge to a wealth of different dishes, harmonizing with the browned bits of crusts, breads, meats, and vegetables at every turn.

Besides being delicious with the browned bits, they also frame tomato sauce quite nicely. Their slight sweetness balances the acidity of the sauce and tends to flavorfully bring out the sweet and tangy components. This combination makes ambers a sure-fire hit

for pizza, with its golden-brown crust and zesty tomato sauce.

I recently fielded a question about whether all beer pairings were "fancy." The simple answer is no, they're not. You don't need to know Maillard to know that you can't go wrong with a well-balanced amber. Consider it one of craft beer's "safe words," one of food's go-to beers. When you want to embrace classic malt character, toasty comfort, and the warmth of a caramel security blanket, sit back, relax, and order up an amber ale to accompany your favorite browned bits.

Red ales are the kissing cousins of amber ales, and you'll likely have a hard time getting a straight answer out of a brewer as to the difference. At times, it may be nothing more than a preference for one style name over another. As a rule, I expect a little less body from a red, and perhaps a brighter sweetness. They might include a little fruitiness alongside the nice round maltiness.

Bocks are in the same boat, as they feature many of the same rich, malty tones. Bocks are lagers, however, so we have our first useful example of the difference between ales and lagers. By nature, lagers' fermentation character is more subtle than ales, thus we'll pick up less of those fruity esters and body. Bocks will share many characteristics of red ales and amber ales, yet with brighter body and cleaner finish.

Dopplebocks are their big brothers, both in alcohol and body. Dopplebocks were known as "liquid bread," and were brewed by German monks to sustain them during times of fasting. These beers' toasty, bready malt character is robust without being heavy. They're delicious accents to Easter dinners of lamb or ham. Their low bitterness also makes them an excellent ingredient in reduction sauces and slow cooker recipes.

Hops: Pales and Pilsners

Spring is a time of subtlety—tender, green growth amidst earthy remnants of cooler times. I find comparing hops to herbs both compelling and informative, and in this case it's also instructional. In the Spring, we're starting to eat fresh foods with subtle flavors, and I look for the same from my beer, especially one featuring hops. I enjoy beers with well-composed flavors and medium to light body that differentiate pales from IPAs (India Pale Ales). Pale ales bring slight, tender bitterness with soft herbal notes and very little citrus. Their aromas are slight and composed, which makes them a delicious companion to Spring eating. Whether you're enjoying them with salads or roasted chicken, or just a sunny day, they bring a brightness to the table. They can typically counter playful heat pretty well, so when I think about things like fish tacos or the jerk chicken we featured here, I think about nice, balanced, medium-bodied pale ales.

Pilsners are similar; as lagers, they're likely to have a brighter body and a cleaner finish. Contrary to what the mass-produced light beers may convince you of, they still have very nice flavor. Their bitterness is typically more of an accent, slightly less pronounced then most other hop-forward beers. These beers are also great for brightness. I like them with crisp veggies like cucumbers and radishes, or simple dishes like grilled brats or a crunchy BLT.

Neither of these beer styles should be limited to Spring, as they'll easily play year round, especially into Summer as the grill heats up and the corn grows high.

Cellar: Farmhouse

Ask a brewer what to expect from a "farmhouse ale" and you might hear, "look for the funk, brother." It's not likely they're expecting you to drink with Sly Stone or George Clinton; they're describing the beer's character and flavor. I figure you may want a few more specifics, although if you have a line on drinking with Sly or George...

I've found that there are few, if any, hard and fast rules or guidelines in the farmhouse beer family. You'll find them in various strengths, intensities, colors, and style names. Each brewer's interpretation through ingredients, techniques, and yeast selection will make their farmhouse ale unique and intriguing. These flavors make for all-around great food beers.

The most common specific style you'll see in this category is saison. Most saisons have a golden lightness to their body and a soft, straw-like grain character, which make them great companions for fish, chicken, and veggies, as they're not likely to overpower their subtle, fresh flavors. Think about how many dishes, especially seafood, call for a fresh squeeze of lemon and a crack of black pepper. Those are all foods that should be considered as pairings for saison, as the flavor bridges are ultimately familiar already—you're just presenting it to your palate in a new way.

Saison is delicious year-round, but it was originally brewed in the Winter and "put-up" to save for the Summer workers in the field, who needed safe, thirst-quenching, and hydrating sustenance miles from fresh water. While I love them with fresh Summer foods, I really enjoy brightening up the end of my Winter stash as we get ready for Spring to roll in.

Wood Aged and Fruit: Coffee and Chocolate Beers

Coffee and chocolate are two ingredients brewers can bring to their beers in many different ways. There's a lot of overlap, because as we've talked about already, these are flavors that can already be expressed from the barley malt, even without the aid of adding the actual ingredient.

This means instead of hinting at coffee flavor with roasty bitterness, the beer may have coffee mingling with the roasty malt tones, adding depth, roast, and even caffeine. (continued on page 56)

Handcuff Soup

FRED RANT

I remember working on one of the first Michigan Brewers Guild conferences, set in a large hotel. We were interested in incorporating our Michigan beers into the dinner, and our account manager scheduled a meeting with the Executive Chef. We would have eighty or so people from more than forty breweries present at the dinner, so we really wanted to do beer proud.

I arrived at the sales offices with another Guild board member; after a short hello, we were ushered into the back service hallways, snaking into the deep caverns of the hotel. The last door opened and we were in a massive kitchen with stainless ovens, hoods, and prep tables sprawling out in front of us. There was a hum of activity, white-coated chefs and cooks at every station, busily preparing food everywhere you could see.

The Executive Chef walked toward us, smiling, and welcomed us to the kitchen. He gestured to a table just beyond the busy hub of the kitchen, set for four with white linen, full table settings, and maybe even a couple of candles. My colleague and I looked at each other, eyebrows raised in surprise; we were just a couple of beer guys here for a meeting, and this was far beyond our expectations.

"Please, have a seat. We wanted to show you what we can do for your dinner. We'll be bringing some dishes out for you. We hope you're hungry!" He smiled and returned to his engine room.

On one hand, I was thinking it was great that this giant hotel thought enough of us tiny little breweries to put out the "impress the client" table. Not to mention, who doesn't like getting fed at a meeting? On the other hand, warning alarms were echoing in my head. "Here we go," I thought.

Now, it may seem a bit egotistical to be pessimistic at this point, but that's where I was. Without a single conversation with the cooking staff, how could they have any idea of what we were trying to do? Secondly, this was 2000 or 2001, so it's not like hotel kitchens and restaurants were all that well versed on local craft beer or well stocked with it yet.

Sure as shit, here it came. Fancy, lidded china soup bowls with lids were delivered to the table. The chef beamed and our account manager looked on optimistically. "I make for you, beer cheese soup!" The chef went on to explain the dish somewhat: he had made it with an imported German dark lager, and he hoped we liked it. So it went with other dishes that might best be described as predictable. Watching the staff deliver on my anxious premonition was a telling moment for me. I felt both frustration at the state of affairs and motivation to change it.

The frustration was that I could feel and see the chef's opinion of beer's role with food. Beer: it belongs next to sausages and in cheese soup; if you're planning a big dinner, put the soup in a fancier bowl. Truth be told, beer soup isn't bad, but it's been done forever and really doesn't showcase any exchange of flavors. Beer soup—the token dish to trot out as proof the chef can cook with beer.

What's more, I felt like we were getting handcuffed, with no potential for discussing beer as a legitimate dinner companion, or exploring new ideas for utilizing it as an ingredient. It even felt like the conversation was being cleverly avoided. Was that table set in the kitchen to impress us or to distract us? Through all the hullabaloo, we never really got to talk to Chef; rather, we seemed obligated to appreciate his generosity and thank him for every course that arrived. It would be rude to do anything else, right? In this particular instance, we didn't have many choices. We didn't have the time or leverage for reproach; we were a volunteer Board of Directors well "out over our skis," trying to pull off a conference for our members without going broke. Lest I sound ungrateful, I must add that the hotel and the chef were gracious hosts of our conference and prepared a nice dinner, with courses we selected from their existing catering menu.

At this point, I realized that whatever I learned technically about beer and food and how to teach it was only part of my path toward change. We, the craft beer world, would first need to change people's opinions about what beer was capable of. Then we could help them discover beer's available beauty and its legitimate place at the dinner table. This attitude adjustment would require navigating our way into kitchens big and small to help chefs discover the world of flavor and potential beer offered. Once professionals included beer awareness when they thought about food and drink, we could move beyond sausages and beer soup.

For the record, a few years later, I participated in a wonderfully collaborative beer dinner at the same hotel and noted the great deal of positive change we've seen in attitudes toward craft beer across the country. It is remarkable how many more chefs, restaurateurs, and hotels believe in beer's potential at the dinner table now versus in 2001. And that's a good thing. I am grateful for the many chefs who have engaged in meaningful collaboration with myself and other beer people throughout the world. I challenge us all, including myself, to keep an open mind, remembering that flavor is without limit. And, in the right context, there's nothing wrong with a good beer cheese soup.

Monkey King Mussels

Mussels are another dish that can be found year-round, but I find myself hankering for them in the Spring and early Summer. You can play with the broth as much as you like. People may debate for or against garlic or tomatoes in the broth, and the fennel in this recipe is my contribution, looking to trigger some of the spiciness in the glass of saison we'll be drinking.

Serves 2 as an appetizer

1 lb. fresh mussels, rinsed and bearded

2 tablespoon butter

Salt

1 shallot, finely julienne

1 tablespoon diced fennel

2 cloves garlic

12 oz saison

3 sprigs thyme

2 scallions, julienne

In a large pot with a lid, sweat the shallots in butter and salt over medium-high heat. Add fennel, garlic, saison, and thyme. Bring just to the simmer, reduce the heat and simmer 5 minutes. Raise the heat to high and add the mussels. Cover the pot and steam the mussels until they have opened, about 5 minutes. Toss the scallions on top and serve with a crusty, grilled bread.

Cacao nibs or melted chocolate are both fair game in terms of upping the chocolate quotient, which may range from subtle to decadently rich.

Coffee beers typically range in style from browns and dopplebocks to porters and stouts, and chocolate beers are no different. There are countless creative interpretations out there, so enjoy the exploration.

This is also an area where you'll see some other typical combinations like a vanilla-java porter or a dried chili and cacao nibs combination. Whatever the case, use the label to help direct traffic via style and ingredients listed, but trust your palate to decide which flavors are most prominent or fun bridges.

I like to use coffee tones as contrast, so I'd consider drinking a coffee stout or dopplebock against any dessert or food I'd like coffee with. I have enjoyed coffee stout with beef brisket tacos or vanilla ice cream. I would also like it with creamy lemoncello tiramisu, using the traditional relationship between a lemon twist, cane sugar, and espresso as my inspiration.

Pairing chocolate beers definitely depends on the composition of the beer. There are a few instances when you can play in savory situations the same way you might with a mole sauce, but the chocolaty chocolate ones are naturals for dessert. I enjoy contrast more than complement here, as you can overemphasize the chocolate, which I suppose is heaven for the chocoholics. I think of what I like with chocolate and head towards dairy, custards, or fruit. Since we love chocolate covered strawberries, we know that chocolate porter is also a tasty friend of the berry.

Enjoy the pleasure of the "freestyle" family of beers and improvise at your leisure. This is an area where it's a bit tougher to know exactly how things will react in advance, so if you're planning ahead for a dinner, it's worth a test run. There are definitely worse things than tasting beer ahead of time in order to plan your dinner.

Bringing Home the Bacon

The Shopping Sacrifice

I can see how it happened. As food and drink production industrialized, our entire shopping experience changed. National efficiencies, streamlined processes, and mass production lowered prices and also created some volume brands. Retailers also focused on volume, built bigger stores, and eventually developed the "one-stop shops" we have today.

This happened as our lives were getting busier. The time we saved going to one store instead of several was quickly filled. Our idea of value, what we should pay for food and drink, quickly morphed into a new standard, to the point that many of us no longer remember the old way any more. We want it cheap, fast, and convenient.

The pendulum is swinging back from those attitudes, and as a people we're starting to miss what we traded away. Slowly but surely, more people are longing for a more comfortable and rewarding food experience. It's as if we are recovering from amnesia, slowly recalling the way we did things a couple of generations ago. Piece by piece, we're putting a lifestyle back together.

I'm not going to scold anyone for wanting convenience and speed. I've been right there with you. We have just adapted to not expecting any socialization at retail. At the age of thirty-one, when I moved from Chicago to rural Michigan, I would just about lose it when the clerk at the hardware store wanted to have a conversation as he rang me up. Doesn't he know I'm in a hurry? I don't want a relationship—I want to pay for my bolts and get on with it.

A lot of that attitude has changed for me over the last decade or so. Sure, I'm still in a hurry sometimes, but I've grown to appreciate the idea of not just tolerating a selective and social retail experience, but actually seeing it as an important piece of humanity.

We can make it our goal to be the fastest and cheapest shoppers in the world. We can also resolve that shopping should be a painful drudgery. But what fun are either of those objectives? Wouldn't it be more appealing to imagine a world where we enjoy the process of selecting what we're going to eat and drink? I mean, first things first: we'll need to enjoy the idea of shopping socially before the reality of it won't seem like a sacrifice.

I'm talking about relatively simple things, but when I'm in my self-focused busy mode, they can seem like nothing but inconveniences. Making separate stops at the local butcher and baker's shops. Scheduling your week around the local farmers market Remembering which days the specialty shop is closed. Visiting a specialty beer store is a different experience than cruising the beer aisle at the grocery store. It's another stop and it won't be fast. In fact, all these stops might cost you more, too.

How is it that spending more money and more time and making more trips is something I can wistfully daydream about? Well, I'll tell you. I imagine talking to the butcher about cuts he'd recommend, or where his beef came from. I imagine him sharing how he likes to cook the sausage he makes, because he likes 'em lean. I can smell the fresh loaf of bread the baker just brought out from the back because she saw me come in. I can imagine the shopkeeper asking me what I'm eating before he recommends a beer. I can hear the farmer telling me about the weather and how the beets get sweeter after the frost as she rubs the dirt from them by habit before dropping them in my bag.

All of these interactions are incredibly appetizing to me in an idyllic way. I don't get to enjoy this bucolic shopping experience every day or week. I tell you what, though: I started to experience it much more often, after the simple realization that I liked it and wanted more of it. When something is pushing me away from this, back into the old way, I just have to ask myself if I have options, whether convenience is worth the sacrifice of one-on-one contact.

And that's really the point at which I realized things have started to change. What used to be considered the sacrifice—extra trips and paying more—became the goal, the lofty aspiration. Rushing through the big store with sale tags and conversation-less efficiency became the sacrifice.

Everybody has limitations of lifestyle, and there needn't be any judgment when we have to do what we have to do. However, I can tell you, if you want more of this reconnected lifestyle, you can have more. I promise.

There's More than Food at the Farmers Market

The next big hurdle I see after deciding to enjoy the social-sourcing experience is not knowing where to start. For instance, I like good coffee, but I feel like a deer trying to cross the highway when I get into some amped-up coffee house with super-baristas. The room bustles with regulars, and there's usually some unspoken etiquette of where to stand when the line is long, or where to self-bus your cup when you're done, or even where the self-serve water is. There are Sharpie-drawn signs everywhere and the names of multi-syllabic coffee drinks written on every surface. It seems like everyone in the room knows how to function in this shit-show but me. At first I feel lost,and then I feel irritated. By the time I involuntarily show my cards with my sarcastic, "Can I just have a cup of coffee?" I end up feeling alienated.

I understand that's how people may feel in a craft beer bar, store, or even the farmers market. Brewery regulars have their own mug on the wall. Farmers market regulars bring their own bags. It's all cozy when you know it, but if you don't know the ropes, walking away and not bothering with any questions can seem easier than risking awkward feelings of alienation.

My goal is to lessen the intimidation factor and help you have a more rewarding experience. If you're already a regular at these haunts, maybe I'll inspire you to lend a helping hand next time you see a wandering newbie. Perhaps we can all help each other learn to use words that sound inviting rather than judgmental or elitist.

Beervangelist's Guide to the Galaxy

I embrace the art of the question. Whether you're in a specialty beer store or the farmers market, I encourage you to ask questions. These shops are where the specialists and hobbyists work and shop. If the clerk doesn't know how to help you, most likely a nearby customer does. You don't even have to be that good at asking questions to start. Show a little interest and let them know where you are and more times than not, they'll want to help. If and when they don't, treat it as discovery—besides getting your questions answered and your fridge filled, you're also learning which shops and which clerks are a good fit for you. I don't recommend ruling out a business just based on one or two experiences with an impatient clerk, but if you find that asking questions is considered a hassle, then I'd move on—you can get that kind of service back at the one-stop shop.

So, what kind of questions? On the food side of things, besides asking about what you're buying that day, think about asking about what's coming next or how you cook something. Not only can you get tasty tips, you'll also get a feel for who people are and how their shop is run. If you're at the farmers market, there are going to be many stands selling the same ingredient, so having a little conversation can help you find your favorites and decide shops or vendors you feel best about buying from. The funny thing is, instead of thinking of this as an opportunity for scrutiny, I've shifted to thinking of it as a luxury. What a treat it is to be able to casually get to know the people raising the food I'm about to buy. If you ask nicely, you'll probably even get to snack on some samples along the way. Start positive and be patient and appreciative of their time—these people deal with many, many customers, so try to choose your moments gracefully.

In terms of seasonal eating and learning what to expect in which season, my knowledge has grown immensely just by paying attention at the farmers market. By the way, I'm crazy busy too, so I'm not a weekly regular—but when I go, I soak it in. Even without conversation, you'll see what produce is rolling in from week to week. In the big stores, it's very hard to pick up on seasons because these businesses ship food from around the world to provide year-round availability. A very convenient thing, when we need it—just not very educational. At the farmers market, you get to feel the seasonality. You can tell when the blueberries are coming in, when they're in their prime, and when they're on the tail end, just by walking the market once a week.

Specialty beer stores have a lot of the same information. You can learn a lot just walking the aisles. Strike up some conversation and most likely you'll run into a knowledgeable enthusiast, whether they're wearing a shop apron or not. What's new? What's your favorite? What would you serve with barbecue? Besides the answers themselves, you'll get a feel for the store and whether it's a good one for you. I've visited thousands of retailers in my career, and sometimes I'm only in their establishments for fifteen or twenty minutes, but it only takes a couple for me to recognize a store I'd like to shop at. I can see their regulars come in and be recognized by name; perhaps they're told of something coming up without even asking, or maybe they share a story about something they drank last week that "you gotta try."

I've been talking a lot about the aspect of shopping, but you better believe that these same places all have good ideas of where to eat and drink. The farmers and butchers know which restaurants are cooking with integrity, and the shopkeepers know where to go to get a proper drink. They're ready and willing to share their favorites via casual and pleasant conversation.

I believe such conversations and a more social context of shopping signals a return to humanity. I know that taking time to converse and interact can feel intimidating, but I've found it all feels better once you start the conversation. Remarkably, what used to seem like a hassle to me is now what I long for when I get pulled away from it. Come on in, the water is fine...

CSAs

A really cool way to get in the groove with seasonal eating, and thus drinking, is to get involved with a CSA or two. CSA is an acronym for Community Supported Agriculture, and they're set up in different ways, depending on the farm and the community. The name and the concept can be a bit intimidating at first; however, I'd like to share some ideas about how to get involved and then how to make it work for you once you're on board.

One of the reasons CSAs be intimidating is the concept of buying a "share." For many people, this requires more explanation. People need to determine whether they're really prepared to invest in a farm and assess the risks and benefits involved. Either way, that sounds a lot more complicated than shopping for groceries.

I look at it as a way for the farmers to have some guaranteed customers for a portion of their crops. The pre-sold dollars and steadiness of a committed customer base really help farmers plan and dig in, especially at the front end of a season. I think people started using "share" because customers are sharing in the harvest of the crop. If a crop does really well, you'll likely get more of it; if a crop fails, you don't get any—but neither of these results affects the price of your investment. Since the farmers can't guarantee much of anything, they needed to express to their customers that quantity and timing may vary. When you buy a share, you're "in" for whatever comes your way.

I encourage you to think of CSA's as culinary subscriptions instead. Like magazines and newspapers, you'll take regular delivery of published goods on a regular basis. The price and frequency are determined at the beginning of the season, but the content will be written by Mother Nature and your beloved farmers. Newspapers don't assure us they'll have a certain number of pages any more than they're able to tell me what the news will be next month. I expect certain sections and topics, but even those aren't guaranteed as part of our commercial exchange. I'm signing on because I trust them to deliver according to their expertise and reputation. I pick my farm shares the same way.

Now, there are a few differences between newspapers and farm shares. I've yet to see a paperboy ride by on his bike and toss my farm share to my porch step. You're likely going to have to pick up your share at an agreed-upon location on a scheduled day. These drop-offs vary but are typically arranged around the farmer's scheduled stops at farmers markets or other large deliveries, so it's convenient and economical for them.

We have a few shares; we pick one up up at our local restaurant, Salt of the Earth, and another at the farmers market. Neither is inconvenient now that they've become part of the rhythm of our weeks. I know of some companies that arrange for farm shares as an option for employees, and the shares are actually delivered to the company for disbursement (a great idea that I'd love to put in place at our brewery). In any case, these are details you'll learn from any farm you contact about a share. (continued on page 68)

Crown Roast / Rack of Lamb

"Earthy" is a word I find myself using more and more as I get deeper into seasonal eating. It's hard to describe in more detail, because it's almost a sense in itself. When I start picking up mineral qualities or other flavors that remind me of the smell and image of good ol' fashioned dirt, I tend to kick around the word "earthy." Lamb is one of those meats that illustrates my point. Good, pasture-raised lamb is really something. The flavors from it are unlike any other meat or protein I can think of. It has a very unique character that is both bold and delicate at the same time. There's sweetness without being rich, and earthy, mineral tones that I enjoy accentuating with mustards, thyme, or marjoram.

Those characteristics all send me to oatmeal stouts and porters as delicious beers for roast lamb—as are bocks and amber ales, with their balanced caramel tones and nutty malt character. These styles accentuate the sweetness and roasted, crusty bits that we all love to savor. Rack of Lamb is an outstanding dish for special occasions such as Easter and New Years Eve. I love the richness and spice brought in with the turnip and horseradish puree.

Serves 6-8
2 racks of lamb ribs, frenched.
1/4 cup olive oil
2 tablespoon stone-ground mustard
1 teaspoon marjoram
1 teaspoon thyme
6 cloves garlic
1/2 teaspoon salt
1/2 teaspoon pepper

Preheat oven to 375 degrees F. Combine oil, mustard, marjoram, thyme, garlic and salt and pepper into a wet paste; use to rub lamb ribs thoroughly. Place in roasting pan or bundt pan, shaping base of ribs into a circle, so the ribs curve outward at the top. Tie with kitchen twine.

Roast for 35 minutes until meat reaches an internal temperature of 130 degrees F. Rest for 20 minutes, which will let lamb finish to a rosy, medium rare.

Mustard Sauce:
2 tablespoon stone-ground mustard

1 tablespoon malt vinegar
1-2 tablespoon fresh thyme, chopped
1 tablespoon beer - amber ale
Pan drippings

While the lamb rests, combine mustard, vinegar, thyme and beer. Whisk in pan drippings from the lamb roast, and taste for seasoning.

Turnip Horseradish Puree:
6-8 turnips, peeled and quartered
1 cup Mexican sour cream
2-3 tablespoon horseradish
4 tablespoon butter
Salt and pepper

Put turnips into boiling water and cook for 10-12 minutes until tender. Drain and return to pot. Add remaining ingredients and mash. Taste for seasoning, adjust and stick blend to desired consistency.

Place the rack of lamb around turnip puree and top with mustard sauce. Slice between ribs to serve.

Roasted Pork Medallions over Barley

There's a sweetness to pork that makes it pair beautifully with fruit, and this roast accentuates that nicely. It tends to pull fruit out of the red ales and abbey ales, making for a very comforting, luxurious meal.

Serves 6-8

Ingredients:

5 cloves garlic, peeled

1 medium shallot, peeled and sliced

1/2 cup golden raisins

1/3 cup dried cranberries

3 tablespoons olive oil, divided

8 leaves fresh basil, or 1 teaspoon dried basil flakes

1/4 teaspoon freshly ground black pepper

Pinch salt

1 boned and butterflied pork loin, or shoulder roast, about 2 1/2 pounds

12 ounces red or amber ale

1 tablespoon orange juice

1 tablespoon dried herbes de Provence (a blend of dried herbs commonly used in southern France. Find it in the spice aisle)

1 tablespoon butter

1 tablespoon flour

Place the garlic, shallot, raisins, cranberries and 1 tablespoon olive oil in the bowl of a food processor fitted with a cutting blade. Cover and pulse until the mixture is coarsely chopped. Add the basil along with 1 more tablespoon olive oil and the black pepper and salt to taste; cover and pulse until the ingredients are minced and pasty.

Trim any excess fat from the pork. Unroll or butterfly the pork and place it between 2 large sheets of plastic wrap. Use a rolling pin or meat pounder to flatten the meat to a 1-inch thickness.

Remove the plastic wrap and cover the pork with the garlic-raisin mixture, reserving 1 tablespoon of the mixture for a marinade.

Roll the loin around the filling. Use kitchen string to tie and wrap the roast tightly.

Prepare the marinade by combining 12 ounces of beer, remaining garlic-raisin mixture, remaining 1 tablespoon olive oil, the orange juice and the herbes de Provence. Place pork in an extra-large resealable plastic bag and add marinade. Roll to press all air out of the bag while sealing it. Place the bag in the refrigerator and chill it for 2 hours or more.

Preheat the oven to 350 degrees F.

Remove the pork from the bag and reserve the marinade. Place the pork, seam side down, in a roasting pan lined with foil. Bake 50-55 minutes, or until its internal temperature reaches 155 degrees.

Meanwhile, bring the reserved marinade to a simmer in a medium saucepan over medium heat. Simmer 30 minutes, or until it's reduced by half. Press it through a mesh sieve and reserve.

Place the butter in saucepan and melt it. Add the flour, cooking and stirring until the flour is pasty and golden.

Slowly whisk in the reserved ale mixture and simmer until the liquid is thickened. Taste and add salt or pepper if desired.

Remove the pork loin from the oven and let it rest 10-20 minutes under a sheet of foil, loosely tented around the pan. The internal temperature will reach 145-150 degrees.

Add some of the pan drippings to the sauce, and whisk well.

Slice the pork into 1/2-inch-thick pieces, and serve.

Barley:

6 cups vegetable stock (Salted water is also fine)

2 cups pearl barley

1 tablespoon butter

Add barley to boiling stock or salted water. Reduce to low and simmer, covered for 45 minutes, adding liquid if needed. Add butter, stir and taste for seasoning and doneness. Simmer to finish and serve.

Fred Bueltmann

Who can you get shares from? Well, that depends too. Some farms have huge programs with hundreds of customers, while others have only a couple dozen, and some don't do it at all. You might see some of them advertise it on their website or at their farmers market table, but it's really as simple as asking. It's most often related to produce and eggs, items that keep producing through a season, so share deliveries will always have something in them worthy of the drop-off. Meat, which is typically harvested less often, is sold with a different type of model, which we'll cover next.

The next big hurdle for people is the challenge of what to do to with food that just shows up every week or two. Nobody wants to waste food, and keeping up with a steady stream of anything can be a challenge. Then there's the ever-intimidating ingredient you have no idea how to prepare. Both of these are real-life challenges, and you'll need creativity to address them. However, instead of telling you that only good cooks should buy shares, I'm telling you that buying farm shares will no doubt make you a better cook.

We talked about walking the aisles of the farmers market to feed your awareness of seasonal foods. Well, when a box of produce walks into your kitchen regularly, you really start to get it. You can see the build-up and the taper-down; you also start to taste the different shades of a season. Buying shares is what really developed my taste for collards and kale. By cooking them a lot in my first season, I not only fell in love, but I also started to recognize the heartiness they pick up in the colder months and how that would shift my preparation. It's important to note that this is not something I knew going in—it is an awareness I picked up as a result of jumping in. So don't sweat what you don't know; rather, consider CSA membership an opportunity to grow and shift what you cook and what you eat.

In the first season of having a share, I noticed that whatever produce I didn't use in the first couple of weeks would start to look a little tired. I'd work to find a use for it, but wondered how my fresh-food program had me spending time on tired-food challenges.

That whole idea all changed by circumstance. We ripped up our kitchen a few Springs ago as part of our ongoing farmhouse rescue. I had two challenges: feeding ourselves and dealing with the shares. We still had food steadily coming in, but no way to prepare it. We had an idea. (I say we, but I'm pretty sure it was Ulla's idea.) On Friday night we'd take our share over to our friends house and make several dishes out of it. We'd pack these in meal-sized containers for the fridge and freezer, which we could heat up in the microwave during the week. A couple of friends joined us for our first "cooking party," and we had a blast. Drinks and conversation flowed, we made four to six dishes, and we ate a couple of them that night. We packed up, cleaned up, and were set for the week. On top of that, we used the share more efficiently than we ever had before. Two weeks later we repeated the effort at another neighbor's, they threw their share into the mix, and we all split up the food. Delicious soups, stews, and casseroles were all hitting the freezer, and no food was going to waste. On top of that, we were really enjoying the company and tasting each other's cooking.

This experience shined a light on how we connect our ingredients and menu choices. Now, whether we have a cooking party or not, I look at what produce we have and think about two types of uses: what can I make fresh, and/or how can I process it? If I'm not going to use all of it right away, I get busy processing it. By processing, I simply mean preparation for longer-term storage. It could be stored as an ingredient, like blanching and freezing greens, or it could head to the freezer as a meal, like a root vegetable stew with bacon and kale.

We grow up as humans and cooks thinking about what we want to eat and then shopping for those ingredients. This practice completely inverts the idea of looking at what you have and then counting on your skills in either cooking or research to help you decide what you're going to make from those ingredients. It's a little more challenging when you're first getting used to it, but deciding what you're going to eat based on what is fresh and what is bountiful changes how you shop and how you cook for the better. CSAs are a great way to connect our eating and cooking habits to our local growers and, thus, Mother Earth.

Buying By the Side

I got into buying meat "by the side" a little bit earlier than I got into ordering CSAs. There are many similarities, both in how they can intimidate potential customers and the challenges they create for cooks. The main thing they have in common is that they can dramatically increase the quality and nutritional integrity of the food that passes through your kitchen.

First off, lets talk about what it means to buy meat by the side and try to address some of the intimidation factor. Buying by the side is essentially purchasing meat based on a portion of an actual animal rather than by individual cuts. "Side" refers to one side of the animal, as they're frequently sold in "half sides." Since animals for the most part are symmetrical lengthwise, this means that each half has the same parts for the purpose of selling and buying meat.

Enter the first point of intimidation: you're committing to all or most of the meat that's contained within that side. Many people don't know the names of all the cuts available from an animal, let alone how to cook them all, so signing up for them sight unseen is a leap of faith, to be sure.

You'll likely pay for a side by a price per pound of "hanging weight," which is simply the weight of your side, before it's broken down or processed. Besides making the purchase simple, this also is educational, as you'll soon figure out why smaller, prime cuts like tenderloin are expensive at the market and items of abundance like ground beef are not.

You'll also likely have two actual purchases in buying by the side. In most cases, you're buying your portion of the animal from the farmer, but it will be butchered or processed by a separate company that you'll pay separately. Enter the second point of intimidation: there are several choices to make for processing. What thickness do you want your steaks? Would you like more roasts or more ground? Rib roasts or ribs? Most people do not know the answers to these questions at the time of their first purchase because these decisions have always been made before the meat made it to the market. One choice affects another, as one cut, such as pork chops, may use what would otherwise be part of something else, like the loin roast. This is easily overwhelming for a novice that has never butchered or ordered this way before.

Either your farmer or processor can help, as they've all handled new customers before. They have guides you can read, and in the end you'll learn a lot no matter which decision is made, as the quality won't be affected by these choices, just the method of preparation. If you have certain favorite cuts that you definitely want, start with those and let the experts tell you how that choice will affect your other decisions.

Finding farms that sell by the side can be a little tricky, because it's often a word-of-mouth sort of deal. The theme of asking good questions remains in place, as I encourage you to ask good questions of the people whom you trust with food. Walk the market and see who is selling cuts of frozen meat. Ask them when and if they sell by the side. Buy some of their individual cuts and try 'em out. Ask them how they raise their animals. Are they pasture-raised, grass-fed, and antibiotic-free? Those are the sort of shifts in raising animals that make it worth-while to invest time and energy in buying by the side. If you're not a farmers market customer or if you're buy-ing during the off season, find a local butcher. If they don't sell by the side, they likely know who does.

With all of these questions, I encourage you to be conversational rather than investigative, even if you're ac-complishing both. In most instances, these people have taken the difficult path of being an independent in a sea of corporate competitors. If they feel as if you're coming in and challenging their methods or assuming they're guilty until proven innocent, you can expect a little defensiveness. Some butchers may not be forthcoming, because you're essentially asking them how you can fill your freezer with meat that they're not going to sell to you. The good ones, however, if approached correctly, will see someone furthering their knowledge of food and raising the bar. Those are customers the butcher would like a relationship with, even if we don't buy all of our meat at their shop. Next tip: support the butcher or anyone else you're grilling for information by making pur-chases along the way.

Ok—let's say you've found a farmer who sells by the side. Now what? You'll need to determine the right size to order; this decision should be based on how many people you're feeding and how much freezer space you have. Also, consider the size of the animal—a half side of beef is equal in weight to a whole pig. Ask a lot of questions and consider splitting an order with a friend if you want to dip your toes in first. Also, realize there is likely a schedule to their season and harvest, so this is not an a la carte method. You'll need to work well into the future, first reserving your side, then responding to a process date when they share it with you.

In choosing your cuts, think about getting tips from someone who eats the way you do. Cooking by the side is a very rural skill, and the habits of people with lots of experience may differ slightly from yours. A rural fam-ily of six is going to make different choices than I would. I look for more steaks, chops, and roasts, while they're

likely to get more ground meat when given the opportunity. They may not even want the livers, while I look forward to making pâté.

Both are appropriate, but the difference is something to think about when talking with your processor.

If you're new to putting up food, you'll likely need to buy a freezer, a very worthwhile purchase that will affect your ability to store all sorts of foods including produce, stock, and even bread. Having a bulk-food freezer is essential to capturing local foods during harvest and storing them through the off seasons.

Interesting side note: most chefs will tell you that the best meat available has never been frozen, and they're right. I can remember feeling a little deflated shortly after beaming with pride over my shift to buying by the side. I heard one of my chef buddies discussing his food program and boasting that he never uses any frozen meat. By asking some good questions, I learned the benefits of fresh-never-frozen, but also recognized the difference between a pro's kitchen and a home cook's freezer.

Busy restaurants with butchering skills can go through whole animals in a short period of time, so there's no point in freezing. They can capitalize on buying from the hook, essentially paying for hanging weight and using the entire animal across many dishes and techniques. These are the restaurants making homemade stocks, sausages, stews, and soups in addition to the steaks, burgers, chops, and roasts that may be featured on the menu. They're putting all of the parts to work, every day and every week.

You, the home cook, do not have the volume to do all of these things in the short amount of time you have with fresh meat. We can use all of these techniques, however, if we freeze. Minimal impact on the meat caused by freezing is mostly offset by dramatic improvement in sourcing.

The next challenge is very similar to dealing with CSA shares. You're going to see cuts of meat you've never prepared before. The process of learning to cook them will undoubtedly improve your skills as a cook, and maybe you'll even find a few new favorites along the way. In our electronic age, recipes and tips are a few mouse clicks away, not to mention that the farmer and processor have been cooking these cuts for years, so they're a resource, ready to help.

Unlike CSA produce, however, all the meat is not sitting in your kitchen, reminding you to cook it. You'll need to peruse your freezer once in a while for inspiration to thaw and cook; otherwise, you might become a vegetarian for sheer lack of planning. I recommend saving the processing sheet you receive with your order. Tape it to your freezer and read it once in a while to keep from fumbling through the frozen cuts with trembling, frostbitten fingers. Also, consider organizing your freezer on the way in. I use plastic storage containers without lids designed for closets and shelves, and I label them. This helps keep the types of cuts organized and keeps them from sliding around the freezer or, worse yet, out of the freezer and onto my toe when I take something out. Also, a pair of work gloves near the freezer goes a long way toward handling these frozen gems with ease.

Buying by the side does more than just improve the quality and integrity of the meat cooked in your kitchen. It also contributes to the sustainability of raising food. If we only ate New York strips, the rest of the animal would go to waste. I like that buying sides creates a natural ratio in our eating habits. Rare cuts are special because there are less of them, and they're treated as such. What I know from this method is that the farmer got paid for the whole animal, and I helped make it all into tasty food.

There are times for exceptions to this ratio. If I'm having a dinner party or event and I want a certain cut that wasn't plentiful enough, or maybe wasn't even included in my side, I head to my friendly butcher—you know, the one we supported while we picked his brain about finding a farmer? Yep, that one. Whether it's dropping by to see what he has or calling in advance to tell him what I'm looking for, I'll be able to cook beyond what I got by the side without sacrificing any of my ethics or quality.

spring

It's Hard to Make it Look Easy

I wish I could tell you there was only one story about me being "in the weeds," the industry phrase for getting your ass kicked in the kitchen. I wish it was as simple as that one time the clock ran out on me as guests began to arrive. But it's not that easy, as it's happened to me a lot over the years.

My ambition to cook for my friends fueled a dedication to the meal that was fierce and persistent. I tackled difficult menus and complex timing to deliver tasty treats to my guests, symbols of my affection and self-gratifying evidence of my skill in the kitchen.

It's both funny and a little embarrassing, however, to imagine what my friends saw as they entered the kitchen during crunch time. As people would arrive to say hello, I'd cut hugs short or quickly set down the bottle they brought and forget to offer them a glass of something wet. Worse yet, I might just mutter a sweaty and distracted "hey there" while my wife was left to handle the greetings alone. The welcome zone of a dinner party is something that Ulla's a natural at, so my younger self didn't see a problem. She has it handled, I'm busy cooking; we've delegated responsibilities, right?

In these earlier days, I didn't even have the vision to shoot for "comfort" or "relaxation" as part of my end result in the kitchen. While I wanted to hang out with my friends, I didn't prepare any time for it until during or after dinner, because before then I was essentially a one-man caterer working his way out of the weeds.

I love to serve food hot and fresh off the stove, so I always timed things down to the minute. I also had a hard time separating prep work into what can be done ahead or, even more delightful, what can be done by others. While I viewed my efforts as examples of tirelessly conquering challenges and working hard to please my guests, I fear my efforts most likely looked like chaos; at least uninviting, at worst downright scary.

Conversation and the bustle of a working kitchen is part of the warmth of home-fired dinner parties for sure, but you need to be mentally present as a host in order to make your kitchen welcoming. These days I try to plan menus and my timing to allow time to greet, share a drink, and generally be present for my guests as they arrive. By getting ahead and thinking beyond myself, everyone can relax and enjoy the casual energy that getting together with friends is all about. Granted, there are still "crunch-time" moments, but it's a lot more natural and graceful to shift into that gear after a smooth and gracious welcome.

It's hard to make it look easy, but it's worth the effort.

Beer-Brined Jerk Chicken

As Spring rolls on, we head to the grill. And trust me, I'm all for year-round grilling, but it's OK, to look forward to spending more time at the grill once the sun is out and warming us up. I've included this beer-brined jerk chicken recipe that my good friend and Chef, Matt Millar and I collaborated on. It's particularly tasty and brings in some mild-to-medium heat that's just enough. Bring out your pales and IPAs, as I think the bright bitterness is a perfect counterpoint to embrace the lively character.

Serves 4

This dish requires some forethought and a few days, so plan accordingly.

Brine:

2 quart IPA or Pale ale

2 quarts chicken stock

1 quart water

1 cup Kosher salt

1/4 cup brown sugar

1 onion, peeled and julienne

6 cloves garlic, crushed

1 cup chopped cilantro

2 tablespoon whole black peppercorns

3 bay leaves

4 chickens, butchered to grill

Place the water, salt, onion, garlic, parsley, peppercorns, and bay leaves on the stove and simmer for 10 minutes. Remove from the heat and chill completely. Add the beer and stir thoroughly, then add the chicken. Let sit refrigerated for 8-24 hours.

Remove the chicken from the brine and rinse under cold water. Pat dry and keep cold.

Jerk marinade:

1 tablespoon ground allspice

1 tablespoon dried thyme

½ tablespoon black pepper

½ tablespoon sage

1 teaspoon ground nutmeg

1 teaspoon ground cinnamon

1 teaspoon ground ginger

12 cloves garlic

2 tablespoon dark molasses

1/4 cup peanut oil

3/4 cup apple cider vinegar

1/2 cup lime juice

3 green onions, minced

1 large yellow onion, minced

3 habenero peppers, stemmed

1/4 cup dark soy sauce

Combine the above ingredients in a food processor and puree until smooth, about 2 minutes.

Pour the marinade over the chicken and refrigerate overnight (two nights would be better), turning once or twice to redistribute the marinade.

Place the chicken on the grill and cook over medium heat, turning often, until done, about 25 minutes. Let rest for 5 minutes, then serve.

Meat Gets a Bad Rap

I'm sick of hearing "That's why I don't eat meat" after people hear horror stories about bad meat factories. It completely misses the point. It's not the lifestyle of eating meat that's the problem. We're omnivores for crying out loud. It's unethical, unhealthy, reproachable handling of livestock and meat that is the culprit. The problem is that people rightfully get so freaked out by the horror show that they want to run away in fright rather than look for choices, or better yet, fight for change.

How perverse is it that somewhere along the line our food industry got so upside down that it became the norm to raise animals chock-full of antibiotics, so the naturally-raised ones were the exception in need of a special label?

Worse yet, think about the reasons antibiotics became so necessary in first place: confinement farming. When they raise animals indoors in extremely close quarters, the air quality and general hygiene "goes to shit"; without antibiotics, animals get sick or die and don't earn their rent at market. With routine courses of antibiotics, factory farms avoid the need to change or improve conditions, as long as we don't mind drugs in our meat.

We have choices, so don't let me scare you into running away and becoming a vegetarian—not that there's anything wrong with that. Animals are supposed to live outdoors, rooting around in the dirt and breathing fresh air. Pasture raising animals eliminates the need for routine scatter-bombing of antibiotics and lets the animals grow up healthy, happy, and hearty. While "humane" seems an odd word for livestock, we can certainly say this is more ethical toward the animal. Just as importantly, it means we have tasty, healthy meat that's not putting drugs into our family's bodies without their knowledge.

It may seem daunting to make the change, but you can start simply—at the butcher, grocery store, or farmers market. Read labels and ask questions so your home can be your first bastion of good meat. "Pasture-raised" and "antibiotic-free" are more important words to me than "grass-fed," which doesn't always tell the whole story. As for "organic," there are plenty of worthwhile, trustworthy farmers who aren't organic by label. Restaurants are trickier, but ask good questions and you'll find out which kitchens are doing their homework and sourcing with good intentions from good farmers.

FRED RANT

Honor Ingredients, Use Technique

I have never tasted a flavorful technique. In fact, I've never tasted a technique at all; absent an ingredients, technique couldn't exist at all. Why is it, then, that so many try to get us to taste it?

In brewing and cooking, and for that matter, any composition, technique matters, but it is developed and employed to highlight, accentuate, or develop an ingredient's flavors. No matter the technique, it can't create flavor out of thin air; it pulls flavor from somewhere within the ingredients themselves.

When selecting beers or creating a menu, I consider which ingredients or beers are at their best at that time and what flavors live within them. What additional flavors will complement or contrast well?

Technique is how we get there, but the path is inspired by flavor and ingredients. Now, we don't learn techniques without practicing them, which needs to happen at times with great repetition. Our practice may be tasty, and many of our guests enjoy being in the process, so by all means practice technique.

Remember, however, it's "technique first" thinking that draws you out of season to inferior examples of ingredients. It's what sometimes makes for odd-feeling, forced menu choices.

Our palate only speaks flavor; it is not concerned about how hard it was, how long it cooked, or how rare the beer is. Ingredients bring flavor, so listen to them and find out what they have to say.

Cooking with Beer

It is important to remember the only time we should cook with beer: when the food tastes better for it. You can enhance pairings by layering flavors that will ultimately make good flavor bridges to the beer you choose to drink.

It must be said, however, that food can taste great and pair beautifully without cooking with beer. It's an ingredient like all others and should be integrated gracefully and with balance. Of course, you could accuse me of misleading you with Beervangelist's Guide to the Galaxy. In fact, it could be considered downright hypocritical to pack a book full of beer-infused recipes and then tell you not to overdo it. I accept this risk, but I want to express that Beervangelist's Guide is geared to enhance your beer awareness, so I've focused on beer recipes as a point of interest, a specialization, if you will. Beer shows up in my kitchen and in my food on a regular basis, but I cook plenty without it as well.

Disclaimer aside, here are some basic tips:

Raw: I consider "raw beer" to be beer that is not heated. You can use beer in aioli, vinaigrettes, brines, and even ice cream floats. These methods leave the beer in its purest form, so it's very easy to taste-test to see if you like it. This is my favorite place for hoppy, aromatic beers, because their aroma stays fresh and accents beautifully.

Heat: Whether on the stovetop or in the oven, heating beer requires some care, as evaporation and heat will start to change the flavors present. The biggest concern here is bitterness. Whether it's a hoppy IPA or a roasty stout, bitterness that was balanced in the beer originally can begin to dominate unpleasantly as you heat the beer. You can prevent this result by countermeasures such as combining other cooking liquids and/or butter. I lean towards low-hop, less bitter beers for stovetop applications, although there are exceptions. Overall, I just try to treat beer gently when heating and taste frequently to learn what works and what doesn't.

Reductions: You can make glazes or caramels with beer, which may not look like treating beer gently. Beer choice is very important here, and I also like to contribute to balance by adding sweetness with actual sugar or another ingredient. Adding butter is also very helpful, as it will reduce the amount of bitterness your palate can perceive.

The recipes in this book should give you a good baseline for how beer can be used in the kitchen. Have fun and explore, but remember that beer's most important role is filling your glass.

Beer and Chocolate

Deep alluring character draws you in; attitude brings you back for more. There's softness, but sometimes you like it rough. Some describe sweetness, but you know the whole story. When you get a taste, you might feel comfort, intrigue, or halting arousal from intense assertiveness. You know you want it.

Some may think I'm talking about soft porn. Others may guess chocolate. Those who know me probably have already guessed beer. You can pick two out of three and have yourself quite a day.

What I love about the description above is that I'm really talking about both—beer and chocolate. There's so much harmony and synergy between the two. If you start with stouts, the parallels are simple yet dramatic. Stouts feature roasty tones from dark barley-malt that emulate the edgy roastiness in dark chocolate. There's typically a soft, sweet center in both as well, framed by the robust character that slows us down and evokes that deep breath after your first sip or bite.

So, forget whatever you've heard about other beverages and chocolate: I'm here to tell you that pairing beer and chocolate will make you swear, maybe even testify. You can start simple and pick dark stouts and porters that feature chocolate-like tones, or even find beers that actually include chocolate, which drives that point home even more. The energy between the similar, complementary flavors is the chocoholic's dream. The bigger the chocolate, the bigger the beer—so save the Imperial Stouts for the big boys. Dive in, submerge, enjoy.

Another fun direction, however, is to take a page out of the pastry chef's or candy-maker's playbook and look for typical contrasting or complementary flavors, which we already love. Think about how desserts are built around chocolate—what flavors come into play? Caramel, nuts, vanilla, toffee, molasses... Sound familiar? They're all abundantly available in beer. The strikingly rich caramel tones in barleywines and wheatwines are killer against big, intense chocolates, and if the dessert or chocolate is garnished with sea-salt? Kaboom.

If you're choosing chocolates which are light to medium in-body, I'd be careful not to overwhelm and look for beers that match intensity. This would be an appropriate time to think about nutty brown ales, which often feature nice sweet malt character and tones of caramel and are not as assertive or bold as the bigguns.

I've included a few of my favorite pairings that I've done over the years with Gail Ambrosius, one of the finest chocolatiers in the land. By pairing to other aspects of the truffles, we bridged to secondary flavors like citrus, ginger, and honey, which created broader opportunities for less traditional pairs like tripels and saisons. Our palates appreciated the entertainment as well as the incredible harmony.

Recommended Pairings

{ Saison — Cointreau Truffle with Candied Orange Peel

Tripel — Lemongrass and Ginger Truffle

Bourbon Barrel Stout — Shitake Mushroom Truffle

Wheatwine — Caramel Sprinkled with Grey Salt

Russian Imperial Stout — Cayenne and Cinnamon Truffle }

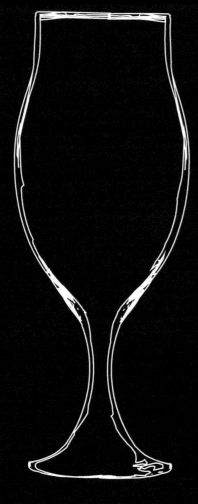

Serves 6-8

Mousse

6 oz. dark chocolate

1/2cup New Holland's Michigan Rum

6 oz unsalted butter in small pieces

4 eggs

3/4cup sugar

1/4 cup. NHB Night Tripper Imperial Stout (or other strong stout)

Separate the egg whites and yolks into separate mixing bowls. Beat the yolks until thickened slightly.

Heat stout and sugar to a simmer, until dissolved. Whisk stout mixture into yolks, very slowly at first, careful not to scramble yolks.

Beat yolk mixture over simmering water with a whisk several minutes until thickened like mayonnaise and hot to the touch. Remove from heat.

Beat yolk mixture in electric mixer until cool and forming a thick ribbon.

Melt chocolate and rum in stainless bowl over simmering water until smooth. Remove from heat, stir in butter and fold chocolate mixture into yolk-cream and set aside.

Michigan Mousse

Truth be told, this mousse is delightful in any season. It's excellent with many beers, and chocolate as well as eggs are seasonless. Raspberries freeze well and are great for sauces like this, when you're hankering for some signs of fresh seasons. This is inspired by Julia Childs classic construct, updated with beer and rum. It is just light enough to be playful, although rich and decadent at the same time. Coffee and chocolate stouts, and other stouts of all intensities play beautifully.

Whip the egg whites and salt until stiff peaks form. Fold 1/3 of the whites into chocolate with a spatula. Fold in the remaining whites, until uniformly integrated.

Pour mousse in dishes and chill for 4 hours or until firm. You may also choose to pour into a stainless mold and freeze.

Remove mousse from refrigerator/freezer, top with raspberry sauce and serve it alongside your favorite stout.

Raspberry Sauce

2 pints raspberries

½ cup sugar

¼ cup Michigan Rum or orange liqueur

1 tablespoon fresh lemon juice

Cook ingredients in saucepan until berries break down. Strain, return to heat and reduce. Adjust sugar to taste, chill.

Summer

Habits of a Good Host

Ever go to a party and feel a little confused about what to do with yourself once you arrived? Or maybe you felt as if you needed something that wasn't readily available, that you somehow didn't feel all that taken care of or entertained. Over the years, I've learned that wanting to have people over and being good at it are two different things. There are certain people who seem to make it look easy, and time spent with them at their place is relaxed, enjoyable, and rejuvenating.

Some of you are probably naturals, while others may be terrified at the thought of having people over. Either way, I think we can all benefit from looking at the simple things that go into making the phrase "a good time was had by all" your new standard.

The basics are the same whether you're inviting a buddy over for a beer, planning a special dinner, or throwing a knock-down, drag-out soirée. Hosting habits transcend all of these shindigs and even apply to taking people out on the town.

Fight within your class. Sharing good times with people over food and drink does not need to be complicated, and you don't even need to know how to cook. We often get the idea that for an event to be special, it needs to be impressive and, most likely, difficult. If we're trying to pull off herculean feats to impress our friends, more often than not our stress can invade the party, literally taking us away from our guests and hosting duties, and delivering some unpleasant energy as well.

You don't have to play it entirely safe, either. Ambition and adventure are exciting, and people love to have something to root for so they can deliver the fun "oohs and ahhs." I encourage you to explore, maybe even a bit beyond your skill level—just find a balance so you can still enjoy the event yourself and be present with your guests.

Shape the event. Hosting a special dinner for a "guest of honor," wanting to try out a recipe, or wanting to compare fifteen different IPAs are all good reasons to invite people over. They're all different, though. How you plan, whom you invite, and even how you choose the food and drink all change dramatically depending on why you're having people over.

If you want to geek out and host a style-specific tasting, or even survey your guests on which pairing they liked, that can be really fun. But if you try to insert it at Aunt Clara's birthday party, you'll likely get some resistance.

Think about who the occasion is for, who you'd like present, and what you think those guests would like to experience, and then create a plan from there.

Invite and inform. Casual or not, when we invite people over, we need to keep in mind that we're letting people know what to expect and how to engage. Do you want everyone there at the same time, or is it a "come whenever" sort of deal? Is it an open invite to anyone and their friends, or is there a specific guest list and number of seats? Do you have beverages or pairings selected, or should guests bring drinks? Are they being fed dinner, snacks, or none of the above? None of these potential responses are good or bad, but when there is confusion or wasted energy, it can take away from the ease of knowing what's going on ahead of time. When this is all done simply, your guests know when to show up, what to bring (or not) and even a little bit of what to expect. These days, we might be inviting via phone call, text, email, or social media, but regardless of the form the invitation takes, the principles of good communication remain important to making it all feel easy.

Prepare your space. We usually live in our space a little differently than we entertain in it. We're set up for the people that live in the space. We know where things are; we have enough coffee cups, chairs, and even a routine for how to keep it clean. As newcomers show up and the numbers increase, the natural ability to hang out in the space changes a bit. A good host looks ahead and prepares for this. We entertain a lot, so our space is fairly accommodating in either setting, but there's still prep to think about before the guests arrive.

It's partly logistics, like storing abundant glassware in exposed areas that are easy to find, having enough extra seats on hand to accommodate, and even creating an obvious, easy space for empties. It's also about ambience, so think about how you can welcome all of the senses. Music, lighting, candles, or a couple of fresh flowers are all simple touches that make a space feel warm and inviting to guests.

Setting the table is an art unto itself. I'm not particularly good at it, and it probably took me a decade to recognize the importance of doing it in advance; however I am a believer. I learned to respect and appreciate this art from many graceful hosts, most notably my wife Ulla. Many a dinner party has felt more relaxed and elegant than it would have if it were left to me alone. What I used to overlook, I now aspire to and admire.

I rely on this step most when a gathering starts to get a little more complex in either menu or number of guests. It allows you an opportunity to set the tone a bit, as you can choose to set it with place settings for each person, or you could set up stations for a tasting party. Your floorplan and gameplan will be a visual cue for guests as they arrive, which helps get everybody in the groove.

Perhaps more importantly, especially for those stretching their skills a bit, it helps you plan where shit goes come crunch time. I remember walking into my friend Laenne's kitchen the day before a big dinner party and seeing that all of her platters were labeled with the menu item they'd hold. Part of me thought that was way too organized to be cool, so of course I teased her about it. The other part of me was in awe. "People think of what dish they're going to use in advance?" I marveled. What a novel concept! I figured it was just a mandatory part of "crunch time" to be holding a hot pan of food with one hand while trying to jiggle serving platters out of my cabinets with the other, as a kitchen full of guests watched. Setting the table is my way of thinking through the evening and taking stock of what I imagine and preparing for it. Simple things like choosing serving platters in advance have provided immeasurable calm during "crunch time."

It's important to note that this preparation idea is not necessarily complex. It could be a ten-minute swing through the kitchen or dining room if friends are popping over for dinner, or it could be resetting the dining room's tables and chairs the day before to accommodate a larger group. Either way, it's simply having the mindset to shift your space from how you hang out in it to how you'd like to entertain in it.

You are not alone: Hosting can seem daunting at times, maybe even more so after I've scared you with all of my advice and tips. In sixth grade, Mr. Garland spent a whole class on the phrase, "There's no such thing as a free lunch." I still carry the principles of that lesson with me today, although that's really a different book. I think this idea, the principle that "You are not alone," is where I feel a bit like Mr. Garland. It's perhaps the most important lesson, yet also the principle I feel you might try to logically disprove the way we tried to best Mr. Garland. I insist that if you feel you are alone, you have yet to look around.

Think about the basic premise of hosting. I think of it as "having people over," "showing them a good time," or "taking care of my guests." Maybe it's my own Midwestern nice, but there are times when I've misinterpreted this and thought that to be a good host, I had to do it all. I would instinctively turn down help even when I was desperately in need, mostly because I didn't know how to use it, but maybe also because I wanted to be the one, the guy who was doing the entertaining.

What I didn't realize at the time was that I was not only missing out on available help, I was also not allowing some of my friends the pleasure of contributing. Many of them, like me, feel better being part of something. They want to do something, whether it's chop onions, set the table, or make us all a drink.

As I considered it from their point of view, I also found the joy of collaborating with certain friends in the kitchen. I learned that hosting is a role of directing and holding space, not about "doing everything." Prep became more enjoyable as it became a unique part of the social experience. Hell, even cleaning up is a lot more fun when it's an extension of the party.

So, whether you're having one friend over or thirty, you are not alone. Think about what you'd like help with, who you like to work with, and who is dying to do something.

It's OK to be selective and even directive. I don't want or like a free-for-all, but I have very much enjoyed loosening my grip and involving more people in the process. It seems backwards, but it is a generous host that knows how to give the pleasure of contributing to the guests who enjoy it.

It's not about you. At the root of good hosting is a generous spirit. Hosting is about giving generously because we want our guests to enjoy themselves. A good host enjoys this act whether anyone notices or not. She enjoys seeing her guests smile and laugh comfortably, and naturally embrace the indulgent bites and sips of a well-prepared meal.

 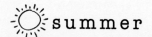

This idea is tied in closely to "You're not alone," because it's often challenged by the instinct to impress that trips us up on both counts. Trying too hard to impress is also what can ruin our timing or make us press something on our guests instead of inviting them in to something we think they'd enjoy.

This affects menu planning in general, but it especially applies to pairings. When I started getting good at pairings, I included them in more dinner parties at home. I could feel a sense of frustration bubble up inside me when people weren't all on the same page and were drinking other things, like wine. I tried to strategize how to insert the pairing more efficiently, but invariably, I found I wasn't really in control. I suppose you have choices at that point. You can increase control by becoming a server and whisking away any drinks not planned by the chef, you can give up trying, or you can loosen up.

I chose loosening up, and the idea was very much informed by remembering that the moment, the time together, the dinner, none of them were about me. It was about sharing a meal together. Yes, I wanted the meal to be delicious, but not at the sacrifice of my guests' comfort or freedom to choose.

The second part is that while it's not about me, it does include me. Sharing my perspective, my flavors, and myself is part of cooking authentically, so I do want to share—I just want it to be inviting. I began to shift how I went about certain menus or pairings. I tried to follow my imagination to what would be most enjoyable instead of what would be most impressive. I found ways to make pairings available, comfortable, and easy to try without feeling cumbersome. This included delivering a few cold bottles and extra glasses to the table shortly before a course and introducing it with something like "I recommend this oatmeal stout with this dish, in case you'd like to try it." This is considerably different from the way we organize beer dinners in restaurants, and I think it should be when we're at home. If you want to have three glasses of different things to drink in front of your plate, I'll bring you the glasses. Indulge, enjoy, and relax, for yourself and as you please.

Warm Welcome. To me, the art of hosting is tying these various ideas together to create a warm welcome. I mean this both literally and figuratively. We should shape, plan, and organize so that when our guests arrive, the atmosphere feels easy. When done well, little things matter, and don't—all at the same time. If you're the cook, think about asking someone in advance to help answer the door and make people feel at home, taking on "front of house," to use a restaurant term. Offering a drink should be relaxed and easy to understand. I like to have a few things picked out so I'm offering choices rather than immediately heading into the ole, "Whaddya have?" conversation. As a cook, I've learned to try to schedule the arrival time and the meal separately so I can be welcoming and receptive when people arrive and still duck into the kitchen when it comes time to plate. Of course, I share that information in advance, inviting and informing them that "drinks and apps are at 6, dinner's at 7:30."

Helping guests "feel at home" is an action that should be natural and generously proferred, even though it takes a bit of work behind the scenes to accomplish. I find the effort to be enriching and rewarding, and so much more gratifying than being impressive.

Eating Summer

"Hey everybody—let's have some fun! You only live but once and when you're dead, you're done, so let the good times roll..."

—Louis Jordan, 1947

Summer is when the good times roll, that's for sure. We kick off our shoes, air everything out, and watch everything grow. The animals are grazing, gardens are hoppin', and with any luck, the beer is flowin', too. As much as we might swear about Winter in the upper Midwest, it sure does build an appreciation for a good Summer day. As I've grown more and more connected to stuff that grows, both hay for our horses or tomatoes and veggies for my belly, my fondness for a healthy and robust growing season has deepened greatly.

It's also a time to cook and eat outdoors. You'll find a lot of my Summer recipes capture Summer foods as well as outdoor cooking. Fresh air, good beer, and the smell of the great outdoors are terrific pairings with just about anything, but I've shared a few of my favorites with you here.

There are so many fresh flavors to choose from in Summer—it's hard to go wrong. It's the time of year we're cooking and preparing the foods with hardly any storage, and that's a joy to be savored. The season changes what I choose to cook and eat, while I also imagine how I'll save some of these ingredients for different recipes throughout the Fall and Winter.

I embrace brightness in beers for Summer, but still enjoy the whole range of flavor. I feel it is a wonderful time for the aromatics of IPAs and the golden beers that I like to drink cold. Citrus and spice are lively and fresh, a perfect complement to hot days and short sleeves. It is an important time to choose well with respect to intensity, as we are often eating lighter foods, which call for more delicate pairing choices.

 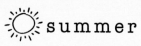 summer

Grilled Tuna with Spicy Radish Slaw

I created two dishes for IPAs from slightly different directions. The seared tuna brings a little bright heat in the Summer, with a slight hand and an exciting base for the acidity of an IPA to play off. I love snacking on a collection of lighter dishes in the Summer, and this is an excellent dish to add to a smattering of tasty bites.

Serves 4-6

1 pound fresh sashimi grade tuna

1/4 cup whole peppercorns.

1 daikon radish

10 radishes

2 tablespoon lemon verbena chopped

1 tablespoon rice vinegar

1 teaspoon sesame oil

1/3 cup lemon juice

1 teaspoon Siracha pepper sauce

1 tablespoon honey

Slice peeled daikon into thin rounds. Toss in salt and set in a colander for 15 minutes or so to extract moisture. Brush salt off with a paper towel.

Pickling brine: Combine vinegar, sesame oil, lemon juice, hot sauce, and honey in a bowl. Add daikon to pickling brine and let sit 20 minutes or more. Remove from brine and toss with sliced radishes, lemon verbena, and olive oil. Correct seasoning to taste.

Trim tuna to desired shape, roughly 2 inches thick. Crush whole peppercorns with mortar and pestle or the bottom of a pan. Coat tuna in pepper and place on preheated grill (or skillet). Cook to desired doneness, leaving plenty of pink.

Scallops with Spring Onions

I love the sweetness of scallops, and I find their gentle flavor and texture to be wonderful companions to Summer. Scallops have that tender, hardly-cooked character that seems whimsical, like a spontaneous skinny dip in a local swimming hole. It's a natural for the almost tropical flavors of fruit that shine through in a hefe weizen and are great with white ales, too. The sweet, creamy wheat and banana notes wrap these soft flavors comfortably and playfully.

Serves 4-6

1 lb. spring onions

2 tablespoon butter

3 tablespoon fresh oregano (alt: 2 teaspoon dried)

1/4 teaspoon dried coriander

1/2 teaspoon dried orange peel

4-8 fresh scallops

Trim and clean spring onions. Saute in butter for 3-5 minutes on medium-high heat. Stir in oregano, coriander, and orange peel and top with hefe weizen, bring to a simmer, then move pan to oven and continue to braise for 20-30 minutes.

Sear scallops separately in a hot, oiled skillet, until golden (2-3 minutes per side).

 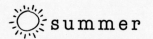

The Great Outdoors

Eating and drinking in the great outdoors is a blissful experience no matter the season. The abundance of Summer certainly offers us the most opportunities to indulge and, at the risk of stating the obvious, I'm going to share some thoughts on how best to bring beer into the barefoot days of sunshine and cookouts.

In the Summer, our kitchens expand to include our grill and the space around it. It's important to remember that "the party's in the kitchen" rule still applies. People will want to hang out where the action is, so preparing the area for visitors ahead of time will help keep you from feeling crowded. Simple things like putting the cooler (or beer fridge, if you're so lucky) in an easily accessible place where foot traffic won't hang you up while you're cooking, pay great dividends. Many craft beers require bottle openers, so hard-mount one on a post or wall near the action and you'll save yourself some trouble.

If you're icing beer outside for guests, keep it out of sunlight or in a covered cooler. The big tub of ice with longnecks poking through the ice is picturesque, but direct sunlight is a threat to beer quality and flavor. Green or clear glass in sunlight can "skunk" beer in minutes. Brown glass protects better than the rest, but keeping it all in the shade or covered is the best policy.

I like to create a self-serve patio when it comes to drinks. I pick a few styles I'd like at the gathering and organize my beer, wine, or spirits just enough so it's easy to see styles and guests can serve themselves. I think it's perfectly natural to welcome someone with "beers are in the cooler," as long as it's not a shit-show in there, where they're going to freeze their hands off trying to find a beer they like. I typically load it light to dark, from left to right. Eventually, as guests bring beer to add to the mix, or bottles start to fall over in the melting ice, the order will be lost; but by that time, we won't care.

Beer is a frequent visitor in my Summer recipes. Brining and marinating with beer are both excellent methods for preparing protein for robust grilling. I also love to par-boil brats in beer, onions, and black pepper before browning them up on the grill. Whether you have it in your recipe or not, keeping a cold beer near the grill is not only thirst quenching, it's a matter of having good form.

When you're grilling meat, fat is going to drip onto the hot coals or burners of a gas grill. These drippings eventually catch fire, flaring up and sometimes turning into a real issue, engulfing our carefully prepared food in flames a bit more intensely than planned. The quickest solution? Douse with a little beer, of course. On charcoal you need to be a bit more careful, as you don't want to soak your coals to the point of putting them out, but addressing the flames with beer takes care of the problem while perhaps adding a little flavor. It's certainly a better tradeoff than using water. I don't always think to load it, (continued on page 110)

FRED RANT

Grills in the Garage

This may be the silliest of my rants, but if nothing else, it's honest. I'll bet you've seen this at some point, no matter where you are in the country—even if you're in a big city and don't have a garage. The garage door is open, facing the driveway. The man of the house has rolled his grill a foot or two in front of the garage and is grilling for his family. You typically see a plate with foil nearby, although I don't slow down enough to get details, as I'm already gawking enough at this point.

You're thinking, a manly man grilling meat in his garage—what's the problem? Once I started to notice this, of course, it got worse; I started to see it more and more, just from being aware of it. When I started to ask, "Why do they grill from their garage?" I started to look for alternatives. Reliably, they often had sprawling back yards with decks or patio doors. In rural areas, some of them even have rolling, hillside views,. But there they are, a few steps away from their gas can, weedwacker, and garbage cans.

 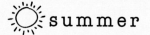

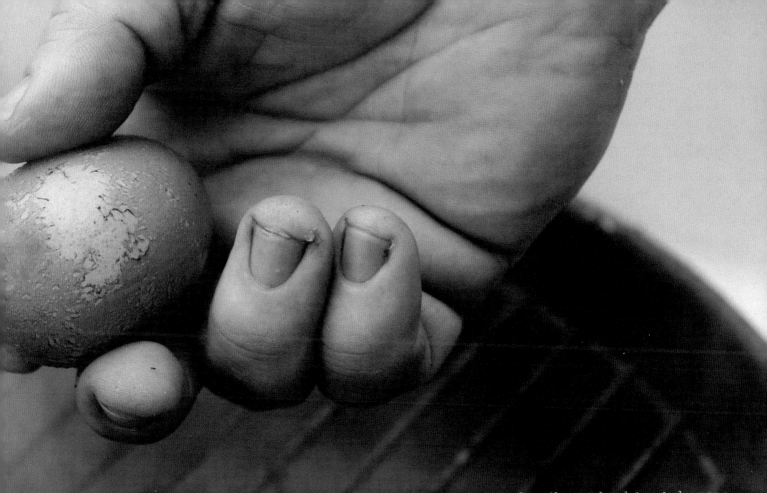

I assume that this habit arose from wanting to keep the grill indoors and use the overhead garage door as a convenience. Although it makes me beg the question, and yes, I'm making broad gender-based generalizations... is the man/grill connection either so strong or so fragile that some will only cook if it involves a trip to the garage for the heavy equipment experience?

Maybe it's just me, as I am sensitive to aromas, but I would prefer a little distance from the industrial smells of most garages. Even if they don't impact the food, garage smells can definitely affect the person cooking, who needs to make sensory-based decisions on seasoning and doneness. Since I also view the grill as an extension of the kitchen and dining room, it would make more sense to be nearer to them, off the back or side, in most situations.

Truth be told, people should grill wherever they want. I feel like I could cook anywhere, and get it done if I were challenged by lack of choices. I implore you to consider your options, though, and give some regard to your cooking environment. Make it comfortable as well as culinary. It should be space you enjoy hanging out in for yourself and guests. Look for options and set your grill free from the garage.

4 slabs of pork ribs

Serves 4-8

Cider Brine

1 quart Michigan apple cider

1 quart amber ale

1/2 cup kosher salt

1/4 cup brown sugar

Combine beer and cider. Add salt
and sugar, stir vigorously until dissolved. Refrigerate until use.

Freddy's Magic Spice Rub

(makes about a pint)

1/2 cup black pepper

1/2 cup paprika

1 cup turbinado sugar

1/4 cup salt

1 tablespoon dry mustard

2 tablespoon onion powder

1/2 teaspoon cayenne powder

Combine all ingredients and shake
well. Store dry.

Boilermakers Ribs

The context, flavor and spirit of barbecue provide a perfect setting
for beer. It quenches your thirst, refreshes your palate, and accentuates the nuances of deliciously layered barbecue. It goes well beyond
the glass as an excellent ingredient for sauces and mops. Beer ties in
tangy flavors and adds a depth, sure to bring the neighbors over when
they catch wind of the tantalizing aroma. A labor of love, to be sure,
but these ribs reward preparation and patience with deep flavors.
Serve with ambers and IPAs.

 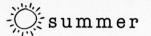

Boilermaker's BBQ Sauce

(makes 1/2 gallon)

3/4 cup brown sugar

1/2 cup Freddy's Magic Spice Rub (or use your favorite rub)

1/4 cup celery salt

2 tablespoon black pepper

2 tablespoon oil

2 medium onions, finely chopped

4 garlic cloves, minced

1 quart home-canned tomatoes, drained

1 1/2 cups cider vinegar

1 1/2 cups barleywine, amber ale or strong malt-for-ward ale

6 tablespoon Worcestershire sauce

2 tablespoon prepared stoneground mustard

2 tablespoon molasses

2 oz. whiskey

Combine dry ingredients in a bowl and set aside. Sauté the onion in oil for 5 minutes; add garlic and cook until fragrant. Add tomatoes and cook 5-10 minutes, cooking off extra moisture. Add dry ingredients plus all other ingredients; stir well. Bring to a boil; reduce to a simmer and cook at low heat for a couple hours. If desired, stick-blend for smoother consistency.

Putting it all together:

Rinse pork ribs; place in sealable container with room for brine. Cover with Cider Brine and refrigerate 24 hours.

Discard brine, rinse ribs and cover generously with Freddy's Magic Rub, working it into all surfaces. Return ribs to container; refrigerate 6-12 hours.

Move ribs to smoker (with water pan), leaving as much rub on them as possible. Smoke with wood chips of your choice over low heat 3-6 hours, depending on how many ribs you're using and how much smoke flavor you want.

Pour a few ounces of beer into a deep enameled pan. Add ribs, cover with foil, and cook in oven or grill a 225 degrees F until cooked through and tender.

Finish ribs on the grill over high heat, generously mopping or brushing with Boilermakers BBQ Sauce, caramelizing the meat and sauce.

Remove ribs from heat. Eat and enjoy!

The Role of Sides

I've taken a lot of inspiration from what we call side dishes. If you think about it, they're the ultimate pairing. Side dishes often make the meal. They complement or contrast with the main course in many different and pleasing ways, and our palate memory of certain dishes is usually about the pairing of both foods together.

You can see many of my favorite marriages throughout this guide. When I'm thinking about creating a meal, I'm thinking about the whole plate. Do I want to accent with brightness like a tangy slaw, a smooth savory base like barley or potatoes, or do I want scrumptious and hearty collards to soak up everything?

Sides are also an extended version of secondary flavors. You should feel free to pair to their available flavor bridges, as they are capable of tying everything back to the plate at large.

I enjoy thinking of our beverage as a glorified side dish. As you consider what you're going to order or cook, imagine your main course, sides, and beverage together in the same moment and allow yourself to exchange options with any of them. Conjuring up these flavor relationship and thinking of them simultaneously, rather than one and then the other, might shake things up a little bit and make the pairing feel less like an add-on and more like a natural part of your meal.

 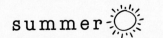

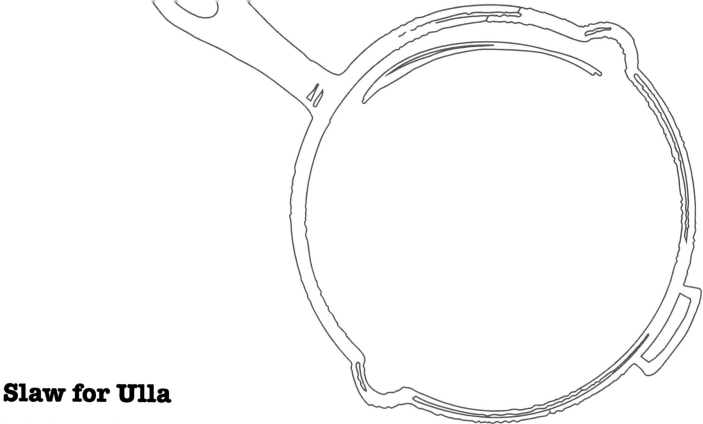

Slaw for Ulla

I enjoy the sport of recreating favorite restaurant dishes, figuring out a way to make them, without the recipe. Sometimes this sends me into periods of repetitive cooking I refer to as "studies." When something is particularly good or particularly new to me, I'll end up making variations of it several times in a short period of time. I dig in deep, pleasantly obsessed like a couple who's over the moon for each other. When I ease up, I feel like I know the ingredients and dish on a very personal, sensory level, and the dish usually ends up as a comfortable part of my repertoire.

Considering the role of sides, as I was getting into making barbecue, I needed to learn a bit about coleslaw. I hadn't ever given it much thought since it was one of those foods that magically appeared next to other things I liked.

This one was the ultimate challenge, with several attempts being summarily dismissed by Ulla's razor-sharp palate. Making several variations and intensely tasting the dressings to try to determine both my target and technique, was very educational. I had learned a great deal about the role and function of a slaw's dressing and once I had mastered this one, I realized I had also developed the ability to improvise many other variations without much trouble at all.

 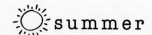

Slaw:

2 cups shredded broccoli

1 cup shredded carrots

1 cup shredded red cabbage

Dressing:

3/4 cup mayonnaise

1/3 cup stone-ground mustard

1 1/2 tablespoon rice vinegar

1 tablespoon celery salt

1 tablespoon onion powder

1/2 cup milk

1 tablespoon turbinado sugar

1 teaspoon salt

1 teaspoon pepper

1 tablespoon lemon juice

1/3 cup olive oil

Combine dressing ingredients in a large bowl and whisk until smooth. Taste and adjust to preference. Focus adjustments on salt, lemon juice, mayo, and mustard.

Add slaw to dressing and toss to coat. Refrigerate an hour or more before serving.

but I like to use a spray bottle full of beer, which makes it easier to shoot under the food and directly hit the fat deposit that's causing the problem. It also delivers less beer to the flame, thus keeping the coals in better shape. Don't forget to clean the spray bottle so it doesn't dry up and clog on you.

Think of your outdoor cooking space as you would your kitchen and provide yourself some counter space that's free and clear. You'll want to stage things waiting for the grill, or set down the platter of finished food. You'll also need a place to set your beer, so plan ahead and give yourself some space. I also like to have herbs growing nearby. I'm horrible at maintaining them, but I love that we have them growing so close I can take a few steps and clip some rosemary, basil, or thyme and integrate them into a dish. Seeing and smelling them not only inspires dishes and pairings, but it also reminds me of the nature of food and makes me feel grounded and wholesome when I cook.

That's also a great reminder to all of us men: don't just focus on grilled meats, as if we had just discovered fire. Summer is the time that fruits and veggies are at their prime, and they should be cherished. Some of them are great grilled, like eggplant and corn, but so many of them also deliver the fresh, bright crunch that is a delightful counterpoint to both the weather and the hot foods off the grill. Bright salads with crunchy Summer cukes, fresh corn, and tomatoes liven up our plates and moods, and they can also be prepped well ahead of time.

This is important, of course, since you've just extended your kitchen and can't be in two places at once. Thinking of these cold counterparts ahead of time will help you time things out more evenly and slow yourself down enough to be a good host. It's also a good idea to remember you are not alone—recruit some help. You'll want some support in whichever "kitchen" you're not in. It's easy to get pulled in more than one direction, so consider your hosting tips and plan ahead so you can enjoy your cookout as much as your guests do.

Drinking Summer

Malt: Kölsch, Golden, and Lagers

I've grouped several beer styles into this season's malt category because they all play in a similar manner. I'm sure there are beer geeks somewhere preparing to correct me, because these beers are built quite differently. Remembering that our palate is not a brewer and that it does not concern itself with such details, we're going to stick to similarities in flavor and when and where we like to drink them.

Kölsch, golden ales, and light lagers all bring a pale, straw colored body with slight sweetness and easygoing intensity. They're lightly hopped, so there's little to no perceptible bitterness. They're clean and refreshing, with subtle biscuity malt character and varying degrees of sweetness.

They're fun with vegetables and fish because they don't tend to overwhelm the lighter, subtler flavors. Sometimes I get a corn-like sensation, in that I taste the sweetness of fresh sweet corn, rather than the canned-corn flavor that can be considered a flaw. That's one of the reasons I'm featuring these beers in Summer: they emanate freshness. I like to think of these as "beer flavored" beers, because they fit the bill on those hot Summer days when you just want a cold, crisp beer.

Hops: IPAs

IPAs feature hops prominently and have become all the rage in the craft word. There are countless interpretations on this style, which vary in intensity and flavor profile. We're going to stick to the basics for the purpose of this section, because I'd rather guide you to understanding how to interpret and respond to an IPA you're drinking than try to academically capture all of the options, a logistical impossibility.

Most IPAs present a floral, aromatic nose, reminiscent of fresh hops. If you don't know what fresh hops smell like, give an IPA a whiff. As you swirl it around, notice the grassy character that seems herbal in some sense. Oftentimes, citrus plays in the aroma as well, perhaps grapefruit, orange, or lemon, depending on the beer and your sniffer.

I often describe this aroma as a warning to our palate. Bitterness is one of those things we're innately concerned about. We don't grow up eating or drinking bitter things, so our palate may express some concern or react defensively. When we take a good whiff and breathe it in, our palate knows what's coming next and has time to prepare itself.

As IPAs cross your palate, they tend to excite different parts. The difference between the beginning, middle, and end is more pronounced than most other styles. There will be malt sweetness underneath, but the star of the show is that tingly, grassy, herbal hoppiness. Whether it seems piney like an evergreen or reminds you of grapefruit really depends on the type and amount of hops in the beer and when they were added. As a consumer, you rarely have this information going in; again, I encourage you to smell, sip, savor, and ask yourself and your palate what it is you taste.

Pairing these can be fun. I like to contrast spicy heat, sharp cheddars, or assertive blue cheese. I also enjoy accentuating herbal and vegetal notes, complementing herb roasted poultry or spicy, bitter greens like arugula.

Cellar: Whites, Wheats, and Weizen

This family of beers is a soft, flavorful treat in the Summer. These beers have more in common than the use of wheat, usually unmalted, to contribute a soft, slightly sweet character to the bread-like malt character. They often express fruity and spicy flavors of fermentation and are usually unfiltered, displaying their yeasty personality through their straw-colored, cloudy, or hazy appearance.

White ales, also known as Wit or witbier, are commonly spiced with coriander and orange peel, which accentuates their playful, fermentation-forward flavor profiles. They have practically no bitterness and very little, if any, hop character. A new style is emerging which is often referred to as White IPA; it blends the characteristics of a Belgian White with those of an IPA, thus introducing hoppy aromatics and slight bitterness to the mix.

Wheat Ale is a widely interpreted style. The beers with this moniker share the overall wheat character, and while some take influence from these yeasty characters, others stay with simple roundness and no fruit-like esters or spiciness. The best way to find out where these are on the spectrum is to pour yourself a glass and taste.

Weizen or Hefe Weizens bring a fair amount of fruit and spice to the game, especially banana with hints of clove as well. They have lively carbonation and round mouthfeel.

I really enjoy these beers with fish and veggies. They are typically medium-to-low in intensity, so they frame subtle flavors nicely, and their spiciness resonates with the seasoning we already enjoy with these foods.

Wood and Fruit: Fruit Beers

Fruit beers can be a bit of a wild card. I encourage you to look past the somewhat dodgy reputation these beers have earned as pretty, light, and sweet offerings geared for palates unaccustomed to beer. Before you open the bottle, you pretty much have a style name, with a fruit or two added, and maybe a brewer's description to help inform your expectation. Raspberry, cherry, blueberry, apricot, apple, and pear are frequent additions. Their range of styles and intensity is vast, from a soft and subtle wheat or amber ale base to a big, banging Imperial Stout, and all points in between.

 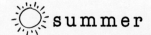

The fruit can be an accent, adding sweetness or tartness, or it can be the star of the show. Either way, they're excellent beers to accompany food because they are quite literally "food beers." Their flavor bridges work very much in the same way that fruits do in their natural culinary setting, so think about where you like fruit and bring on the beer.

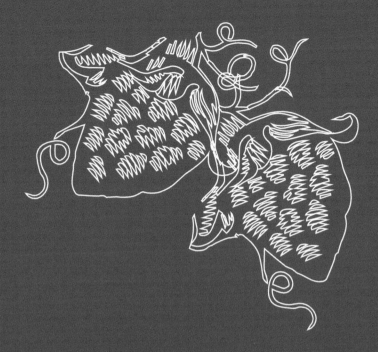

Hops

SOMEWHAT TECHINICAL

I want to share some tips on reading labels that may help you refine your choices within the styles of beer that feature hops. Like most other categories, there aren't hard and fast rules, and one hop variety may have several different characteristics depending on whether it was just for bittering, flavor, or aroma.

If you see the style designations English-Style Pale Ale or India Pale Ale, you can expect them to lean towards more herbal and earthy characteristics. They may include hops from anywhere, but the style itself calls for these flavors more than citrus. Hops that may indicate this style are Fuggles, Kent Goldings, and Northern Brewer.

American-Style Pale Ales and India Pale Ales, on the other hand, are expected to feature citrus-forward, fruity, and piney flavor and aroma. They may vary in intensity and in hop variety, but, as a rule, they tend to focus on those citrus notes. If the style is identified as American, look for hop references like Centennial, Cascade, Citra, or Simcoe. These are popular American-Style hop varieties, often identified in descriptions or even beer names, and they're clues that citrus and grapefruit flavors in aromatic, floral beers are on the way.

I'll reiterate my flavor first perspective that one does not need to know about hops to enjoy a beer. However, understanding a few of these basic directions might help you navigate well within the wide range of pales and IPAs.

My Beer is Not a Number

As mentioned in the "communicate instead of impress" rant, the Internet has brought great change to our culture. Amongst many shifts is the instinct to immediately judge products or experiences and express these opinions to the universe through many opportunities on the web, both organized and casual.

I may be stating the obvious, as this has not been a subtle shift. Businesses have been built around this trend and our apparent need to express ourselves critically. Whether it is book reviews on Amazon, restaurant reviews on Yelp or Trip Advisor, or beer reviews on Beer Advocate and Rate Beer, consumers have a portal to share what they think, early and often.

This habitual immediacy is seen in other Internet trends like status posts, tweets, and check-ins, but with the reviews, there's something different. They're pushing us to quantify experiences and calculate value both immediately and fairly critically.

For a number of reasons, I'm happy there are growing communities talking about food and drink. However, I do feel this somewhat unchecked descent into a world of constant and instant criticism has some problems. I fear that in this incredible time for food and drink, instead of consumers and producers growing together and celebrating the incredible improvement we've seen in the choices available to us, we're seeing a divide grow between us that takes away from the community we could have.

I think we are growing impatient. I agree with the premise that bad service or a bad experience can be shared productively to assist people with their buying decisions. The thing is, we also need to give the story some space to play out. It seems a cliché, but rushing to judgment is not only impatient, it also likely doesn't tell the whole or accurate story.

I get that the prolific nature of reviewing needs some structure to organize all of the content. Thus, various types of ratings get put in place so you can sort through and see what shows at the top. After being around this a long time, I just find it impersonal. Eating and drinking is a romantic experience for me. I like the arc of flirtation and expectation. I want to get to know a bar by hanging out for a while, and I'd like to savor the experience of a chef's food several times before having to decide exactly what I think, or how many stars I'm going to give a dish. I'd like to get to know a beer or a spirit in the same way, connecting to it openly rather then determining it's worth with a cold, analytical assessment. What would we think of a person who rated his or her lovers and kept a sortable database ranked by attribute or total score? To describe rating as "impersonal" in that context would seem overly kind, don't

 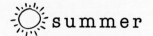

you think? And why can't we strive to have a relationship with flavor, food, and drink that's every bit as personal and respectful as human relationships?

Part of the gap with numbers for me is about preference, and part of it is "time and place." A 99% or five stars do not mean the place or the beer is appropriate for everyone. It lacks the contextual information that would match style and intensity to people's preferences. It might even obscure valuable information from the potential drinker by telling one story by numbers and not revealing the subtext of its deeper flavor or character. Look at the lists of "highest rated" beers of the world: they are not congruent with what we as a culture are drinking on a day-to-day basis. While these lists may demonstrate some prowess in brewing, they won't help you select your next beer.

Precise, unbiased, analytical tasting is a valuable tool in judging beer. It requires a fair amount of preparation and coordination, because our brains can create perceptions from preconceived ideas, memories, or predictions. Professional judges and quality control professionals work hard to separate their brains from outside influence, often tasting blind and with established control settings. It's a completely different experience from what most of the connoisseurs and home-reviewers are looking for and, while very informative, it's far from relaxing. Without these controls, however, the overall data from these sites may be interesting, but from an analytical point of view it's a biased sampling and therefore irrelevant.

There's also something to be said for drinking the beer you're with. There's a time and place for everything. I've grown pretty fond of the canned, domestic beer that is found in the coolers of our neighbors who volunteer to help us put up hay. When I'm coming off a hay wagon hot, sweaty, and tired, it really hits the spot. There are several reasons that it is enjoyable to me in that moment, but all of them defy whatever judgment would have been bestowed on the beer itself by our craft community.

So, I say share all the information you care to, about beer, food, restaurants, or bars. Embrace the community that's been formed around enjoying our newfound abundance in flavor. Take it all with a grain of salt, however, and eat and drink whatever and wherever you'd like. Prepare to dismiss any and all judgments or prejudice that may come your way. I reviewed judgment, and it tastes like shit.

 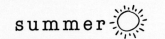

The Art of the Picnic

I didn't respect the art of the picnic when I was a kid. I don't know if I was just too cool for it, or if it had something to do with the practicalities of being the youngest in a large family. If we were packing food to go, it was about logistics and getting people fed.

A life on the move, and meeting so many wonderful friends around the world, has taught me to appreciate the skills and sensibilities of the gypsy gourmands who know how to delight your senses and serve as good hosts, no matter where they are.

When I think about the art of the picnic, I'm not limiting this to the idyllic checkered blanket on a grassy knoll with a basket, chirping birds, and matching napkins. I imagine being outdoors and finding ourselves hungry, when a friend reaches into their rucksack and pulls out a 750 ml. saison, an aged salami, crusty bread, and a corkscrew. It takes a planner to live for unplanned moments. These moments of surprise decadence and rustic refinement are not only charming, they provide rich sensory memories.

Whether we're headed for lawn seats for a concert or hitting the trail for a hike or a ride, we can use our foundation of hosting and pairing skills to create wonderful moments for ourselves and our friends. Picnics are for sharing. Think about how to get more out of the experience by bringing along things that are fun to share. Large bottles, growlers, or cans go further with less waste.

If you're essentially "car camping" with large coolers and ice, your options increase. Packing containers of prepared foods, dishes, and ice-cold beverages are a reality you can put to work. This means you can pack more perishables as well as foods like salads and cole slaw that require plates and forks.

When it comes to packing beer for the backpack, or more remote settings, I like to pack beers that I enjoy at any temperature, especially if it's going to be a long day. Remember that cold becomes cool becomes "cool-ish." Light lagers, pales, and IPAs are excellent when they have a good chill, but sometimes feel a little out of balance when they're heading towards warm. Typically, malt and fermentation character will become a bit more robust at warmer temperatures. If these flavors are a significant part of the beers original signature, it feels less out of place for them to become more prominent. Saisons, tripels, porters, and stouts are beers that I enjoy at almost any temperature, so the thought of them coming out of a warmish backpack is comforting and appealing to me. This list will change for each palate, but if you're packing a bag, think about which beers or flavors you'd drink off your kitchen counter, and pack those.

The same holds true for food. You're not just thinking about foods that won't spoil; you're thinking about crafting an experience. But if you're in a more nomadic mode, how about cleaned and trimmed radishes and

 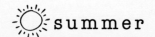

carrots, along with a chunk of aged cheddar and tasty smoked whitefish? These are aged foods that have been prepared for storage. The cheese won't last forever, but it will be enjoyable as it warms and softens. These are also foods that can be shared with your hands and eaten bite by bite. I love the image of sitting in the dirt, slicing cheese with a pocketknife and handing each slice to a different friend, while they pass hunks of torn bread around.

This is another section where specific tips or lists would really contradict what I'm trying to express. What I want more people to realize is that flavor, culture, and comfort from food and drink are always available with a little thought and creativity. You don't have to be on the trail to provide for yourself or travel mates. A train car, a car ferry, or a hotel room after a long day are places often in desperate need for thoughtful, restorative moments that food and drink can bring.

While we live in a time of great choices, they are not always convenient or near us. Besides some exceptions where bringing food or alcohol is prohibited, it is our creative preparation and decisions that make the difference between feeling stranded in a world of poor choices and feeling that "this is the life." We can pack our bag and provide choice, flavor, and sustenance. We can be the gypsy gourmands who make someone's day when we offer them a bite or sip far beyond their expectations in an otherwise desolate moment.

Dragon's Smoked Trout

The Dragon's Smoked Trout combines many of my favorite things. I'm a big fan of leeks and mushrooms as well as smoking things with barrel wood. A few years back, I wanted to feature the regional fish of the Great Lakes in an article I was writing. I was tired of the classic and tasty but often repeated fish and chips options. I've seen a million beer batters and tarter sauces, typically paired with lagers and pale ales. I wondered how I could bridge to earthier flavors to both provide some variety as well as develop more pairing opportunities.

I imagined the umami characteristic of smoke and mushroom, that almost indescribable sensual flavor that most often comes up as "earthy" to me. I was a little unsure of myself, because I'm not the strongest fish-guy out there. I enjoy cooking it, but it's not my wheelhouse. Almost unbelievably, this recipe came out of my head and hit the plate without any revision. The only challenge was deciding what to pair with it, because it seemed to go well with several different beers. I liked it best with the amber styles and bocks, and it will also go nicely with golden ales and kölsches of Summer.

Dragon's Smoked Trout

Serves 8-10

4 trout fillets

4 tablespoon butter, divided

Salt and pepper to taste

Fresh basil, thyme, and marjoram sprigs (3 or 4 each)

4-6 leeks

2 cups button mushrooms

1 head garlic, peeled

1/4 cup Dragon's Milk Ale barrel-aged stout

1/4 cup cream

1/2-1 teaspoon balsamic vinegar

Start coals; when coal bed is established, add Dragon's Milk barrel-wood (or substitute oak chips soaked in beer). Target cooking temp of 225 degrees F. Using a food processor, thinly slice leeks before soaking in water to clean; remove and dry with kitchen towel. Slice cleaned mushrooms and garlic in food processor as well.

Rub cut side of trout with 1 tablespoon butter; season liberally with salt and pepper. Layer 3/4 of leeks, garlic, and mushrooms atop trout; season again with salt and pepper. Arrange herb sprigs on smoker rack; top with prepared trout. Smoke for 50 minutes to an hour; when done, remove trout to rest. Save herbs.

Dipping Sauce: While fish rests, melt 3 tablespoon butter in a saucepan; add remaining leeks, mushrooms, and garlic. Season with salt and sweat until vegetables are tender. Strip herbs from smoked sprigs (about 1/2-cup total); add to saucepan, followed by Dragon's Milk and cream. Simmer 15-20 minutes. Add balsamic vinegar and stick-blend to even consistency; correct seasoning to taste.

Serve trout warm or cold with dipping sauce.

Beer Fest Pretzel

Summer is the time for beer festivals. And, if you don't know this, people at beer fests like to wear necklaces they can eat. I suppose it's all about keeping both hands free for sampling beers. Over the years, I've seen this trend develop from pretzel necklaces, to a shit-ton of pretzels necklaces, to necklaces with those travel packs of cheese, sausage, and jerky. It's certainly playful, but I noticed the discrepancy between the quality of craftsmanship in the beer being sampled vs. the commodity foods dangling around the necks of our spirited fest goers. Could we do better? The beer fest pretzel is my answer. It's also delicious as little pretzel beads in a bowl as an appetizer for your cook-out, so don't feel pressure to wear it. These necklaces are built for easygoing pale ales.

Beer Fest Pretzel Necklace
(About 50-75 pretzel "beads")

4 oz. water

8 oz. amber ale (Sundog, of course)

1 tablespoon turbinado sugar

2 teaspoon kosher salt

1/4 oz. active dry yeast

2 oz. unsalted butter

4 cups all-purpose flour

Vegetable or olive oil for bowl, board, and pan

3 quarts water, combined with 2/3 cup baking soda

Egg wash: 1 egg yolk and 1 tablespoon water, beaten together

8 oz. stone-ground mustard.

Combine water and beer; warm to 115-120 degrees F. Transfer to mixing bowl; add sugar and salt, then top with yeast. Let sit for 5 minutes, until foamy.

Add butter; mix with dough hook on low, adding flour gradually. Mix 4-5 minutes, gradually increasing speed. Move dough to lightly oiled bowl, cover with plastic, and let rise 1 hour, to double its size.

Preheat oven to 400 degrees F. Bring water and baking soda to a boil.

Roll out dough on lightly oiled surface to 3/4-inch thickness. Cut into small squares; pinch one corner to create a "tab." Drop each square into boiling water for 30 seconds to 1 minute; remove with slotted spoon.

Inject mustard into pretzels with food syringe. Toss with egg wash, then with kosher or pretzel salt. Place on parchment-lined, oiled sheet pans; bake for 10-15 minutes, until golden brown.

Cool on rack. Thread kitchen twine through tabs and tie into necklace. Hold in paper bags until beer fest morning. Share carefully.

 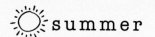

Beer and Cheese

I have fallen in love time and time again over a hunk of cheese and a glass of beer. I have also used beer and cheese pairings to teach the essentials of pairing more times than I can remember. There are several reasons I encourage people to indulge and explore the world of beer and cheese.

Simple and Easy: You don't need to cook or attempt to tackle pairing a full-blown meal to dip your toes into the art of pairing. A few interesting cheeses and a knife and you're on your way. I'll provide some tips and suggestions here, but I want you to recognize this as a very fun place to experiment. It is as easy as picking up a range of cheeses from the market; you don't even have to know what they are or what you think will work to try a bit of this with a sip of that. By tasting around the board and having various styles of beer to choose from, you can dabble to your hearts content, with very little risk or prep.

Pairing Basics: Cheese offers a range of flavors that play well with beer. You can have fun matching intensity, as cheeses range from subtle to extreme. The Four Cs are all available; you can complement, contrast, cleanse, and create, all based on your choices in beer and cheese. You will find harmony and some combinations that artfully pull secondary flavors forward, delighting your palate with fresh perspective and intrigue.

Showcase for Beer: Cheese has many similarities to beer, and it benefits from the culinary flavor bridges available in beer. Whether you're just getting started or feeling comfortable while you deftly replicate your greatest hits, the experience is a showcase for beer's attributes. The roast, caramel, and nuts of malt-forward beers, the herbal aromatics and citrus of hoppy beers, the spice and fruit from the cellar, and oaky, vanilla-laced, barrel-aged flavors are all at home with the world of cheese.

This is another soapbox moment for me. I find it hard to believe how many people are surprised or even doubtful to hear about beer and cheese going together. I guess it's like knowing the best-kept secret, but I encourage you to use it like a not-so-secret weapon for hosting or educating yourself through tasting and exploration.

I have fond memories of one of my first forays into developing my own palate awareness for beer and cheese. I wanted to offer cheese pairings to a certain market, an account of the brewery. I bought about a dozen cheeses out of their cheese case and invited a few friends over for a Super Bowl Sunday get-together. I wanted to enjoy it as a social event, but also wanted to collect some opinions, so I made each person a set of notecards, one per cheese, that they could make notes on. I listed which beers I thought would go well with each cheeses on their cards, but left blank spots for tasting notes and other beers they might end up trying with them. I put all the cheeses out on a few boards, with labels on toothpicks so we'd know which was which. I had several bottles each of about eight different beers. We started out very serious, gathered around the island, tasting and sipping. Eventually, we were sitting around the coffee table, engaged in deep debate about beers and cheeses, digging

 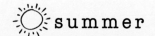

into slight nuances or declaring personal favorites. When someone tasted something entirely differently than I had, I was compelled to go back and try it again.

When we were done, I had a stack of notecards that I could read through to look for trends or favorites. I could compare other people's experiences against mine and browse for characteristics or bridges that seemed more universal than others. From there, I was able to dial into six or seven pairings that seemed to make the most sense and then re-taste in order to hit my original objective of providing pairings to the market.

Think about the experience or process we took to get there for a minute. I entertained and fed a party of six without cooking or even declaring what pairings they "had to" have. We were talking, laughing, and sharing in the most enjoyable way, and people engaged as much as they felt like, sometimes just sitting back and enjoying the moment. It is an experience that not only informed our palates but also my sense of space and structure. We learned more as a group because we had room to explore and enjoy. True to form, the beer and cheese were the stars.

Here are some beer and cheese basics, which I encourage you to disregard at your earliest convenience. I have chosen some cheese styles that I believe should be fairly available, no matter where you are. There is beauty in the reality that the flavors of each style will change based on the grass the cows and goats eat in your area and the method of the cheese makers. I hope that these notes give you an idea of some of the bridges that I enjoy riffing on when tasting cheeses and recommending beers.

Beer and Cheese

Fresh Chevre (goat cheese). Tangy and slightly nutty, chevre will brighten ambers and other malt-forward beers, while the beer's malt frames the cheese nicely. Styles: Ambers, bocks, amber lagers.

Raclette (semi-soft, cows milk). Mild, earthy notes in the cheese call for similarly subtle, earthy beers. Bring light malt character with low hop profile. Styles: kölsch, helles, light lager.

Peppercorn (semi-soft, aged goat or cow). Big enough for bright, bold beers with complex sweet and spicy profiles. Styles: Saison, tripel, hefe weizen.

Aged Cheddars (semi-hard, cows milk). Sharp cheddars, with hints of salt from their hidden gems, AKA calcium lactate crystals, contrast nicely with the citrus of assertive, yet balanced hoppy beers like pales and IPAs. The creaminess can pull forward the malt character, typically making the beer seem lighter and more agile. Styles: Pales, IPAs

Gruyere (semi-hard cows milk). A Swiss mountain cheese, this is known for it's balance between its soft, rich creaminess and a pleasant nuttiness. I find pairing it to malty beers that also have some nuttiness to be a delightful complement. The otherwise secondary flavors harmonize, making the experience more complex as they step forward. Styles: Brown ales, amber ales.

Gouda (semi-soft cows milk). Creamy and nutty. Head toward caramel tones in beer and avoid overt bitterness. Match intensity by looking for medium- to light-bodied beers with clean finishes. Styles: Amber Ale, bock, amber lager.

 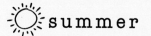

Double Crème (soft cre'me-ripened cows milk). These cheeses change with their age. From slightly tight and springy to soft and gooey, they evoke rich dairy tones. They're often sweet, with soft and pleasantly musty tones. They benefit from caramel and depth of body that allow the cow's milk flavor to be at its best. Styles: Abbey ale.

Triple Crème (soft-ripened cows milk). Silky-smooth creaminess, complex aroma with soft, rich payoff inside. I love the contrast of dark roast against these indulgent cheeses. Cream and coffee, chocolate and vanilla; it is decadence. Style: Oatmeal stout, stout, porter.

Blue (semi-hard, cows milk). Like any cheese, there are wide ranges of blues out there. Thinking of an assertive, aged blue, all Four Cs typically engage. It's fun to contrast with either the cleansing bitterness of hops or the big, bold edginess of roast. Match intensity, which typically means go big or go home. If you have more subtle blues, keep the flavors in mind while you dial back the intensity of the beer. This is a wheelhouse flavor for beer, which you can pair several different ways. Styles: IPA, Imperial IPA, barrel-aged stout, Imperial stout.

Grilled Halloumi

I think it was Food Dance in Kalamazoo that first introduced me to halloumi. It's a Greek white cheese packed in a brine that is like magic. It defies logic on the grill, as it does not melt through the grates, but instead wears the grill marks like deliciously crispy cheese tattoos. I'm not even sure how it's possible, but once I was turned on to it (thanks Robb), I was off and experimenting at home. I love halloumi's bright, slightly salty character and how it plays off the fresh Summer flavors of corn and tomatoes. All of this is delightful with kölsch, as the salt and corn dig in and bring the sweet malt character forward. The same would be true with just about any medium-bodied golden beer with a low hop profile, but kölsch is my favorite and the beer I designed this dish around.

 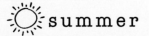

Grilled Halloumi

Serves 4-8

2 packs of halloumi cheese, packed in brine

Corn Salsa:

1/3 cup diced shallots

1/3 cup fresh sweet corn kernels, sliced from cob

1/4 cup fresh tomatoes, diced

1 tablespoon sesame sunflower oil (or other bright, light oil)

1/4 cup chopped cilantro

Salt

Pepper

Juice from 1/2 lemon

Combine shallots, corn, and tomatoes in a bowl. Toss in oil and taste for seasoning, add cilantro to preference and re-toss. Place halloumi on a pre-heated grill. Turn after 3-4 minutes, watching for browned grill marks. Remove to plate and top with corn salsa.

Honey Blue Rotisserie Chicken

Summer is the time to buy fresh chickens from your local growers. You can freeze them for the off-months, but bringing a fresh, never-frozen bird home from the market and grilling it that night is a treat for the senses. Culturally, we have grown accustomed to chicken that is a shadow of its potential self. Fresh, free-range quality chicken, cooked well so it's moist and tender, can change your entire understanding of what chicken is. It will spoil you, and probably reduce the number of places you order chicken from, but maybe that's a good thing.

You can go much simpler than the dish I created here and be quite happy. Herbs and citrus will get you there. For this dish I combined several of my favorite bridges for hops: herbs and citrus, as well as blue cheese and honey. I hope you'll find that this dish hits most, if not all, of the Four C's, with a range of IPAs from medium to assertive.

Serves 4-6

1 whole chicken

1 lemon

Salt and pepper

4 tablespoon butter, softened

3 tablespoon honey

1 lb. pasta, fettuccine

2 cups fresh basil, chopped

1 teaspoon fresh lemon zest

4 tablespoon olive oil

1/2 cup blue cheese

Preheat rotisserie-equipped grill. Rinse chicken and pat dry. Cut lemon in two and insert into cavity of chicken. Mount chicken to rotisserie skewer and truss to hold wings snugly. Season chicken with salt and pepper. Mix butter and honey well and divide in half. Brush one half onto the chicken, working to rub it into all nooks and crannies. Set skewer into hot grill and begin rotating.

Melt remaining honey butter until liquidified and set near grill. After 30 minutes, baste chicken occasionally with remaining honey butter. Begin checking temperature at 50 minutes, and continue until done. Remove and rest 30 minutes or more on a slotted board. Carve and slice into bite-sized pieces.

Start water upon removal of chicken. Boil pasta in salted water until al dente. Set chopped basil and blue cheese in large enough bowl to toss pasta. Drain pasta and add to basil and blue cheese, tossing to coat. Add lemon zest and chicken and toss again, adding olive oil if you want to loosen it up.

Better Make Sure It's Done

I remember trying to cook spaghetti as a freshman in college. I was anxious to take advantage of the kitchenette in the common hallway—a stove and a sink, I think. I didn't have much skill or awareness, besides my breakfast basics, but I'd bought dried spaghetti and jar of sauce, so how hard could it be?

It's not hard of course. I had a box with instructions, but whether I had a timer or not, somehow or another I had some consternation about the question, "how will I know when they're done?" I did what any resourceful teenager does: I asked the other eighteen-year-olds who didn't know what they were talking about for advice.

Of the few that I wrangled, most shrugged their "don't knows" and moved on, surely on their way to the cafeteria or to order up some pizza. However, my Italian RA had a suggestion: his Mom always told him to throw a noodle on a wall, and if it stuck, it was done. Perfect—there's a test.

So after eight or nine minutes went by, I'd pluck a noodle from the boiling water and fling it on the wall behind the stove. It would cling there for a second before peeling off and sliding down behind the stove. I waited a few more minutes, and after a few tests it held long enough that I was content I had followed the rule. The Italians had spoken, I had listened, and now I had safely prepared spaghetti noodles. I warmed the sauce, combined it with the pasta, and shook the parmesan dust from the magic green container to top it off.

I'm sure you can imagine there are a few things about this story that reveal a shift in food philosophy. The part that shines brightest for me is not the bottled sauce or "cheater" parmesan—it's the anxiety over knowing if something's cooked long enough. I was insistent that I have an answer, as if proper "doneness" of noodles was a matter of health and food safety. Think about it: I was cooking dried pasta—there's no blood involved. The only thing stopping us from eating it out of the box is unpleasantness. Apparently, I wasn't alone, as my pleas were answered with an established "trick" to ensure doneness.

I listened, too. For a couple of years, the walls behind the stoves in my various apartment kitchens all had pasta semi-permanently adhered to them, alongside some streaks left behind from fallen soldiers.

Years later, I read something about cooking noodles al dente and how to gauge it by sampling the noodle. They talked about the springiness of al dente, and how it was past the

 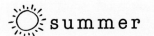

crunch of an undercooked noodle, yet before the soft, mushy aspect of overcooked noodles. Besides learning a bit about noodles, another point struck home, perhaps embarrassingly so. "Oh… You can taste it to see if it's done." Another novel concept.

I started plucking noodles from the pot and taking a bite instead of throwing them against a splattered wall. I noticed the texture and began to realize that the only question I needed to answer was whether I thought it would be pleasant to eat. It was pasta, not chicken—I wasn't risking a global salmonella incident.

And there's the rub: as time went on, I started to recognize a theme from my childhood. We had been unknowingly taught to fear food. I didn't fear it when it was handed to me—I ate everything and anything—but the idea of making or cooking anything had this idea of "cook it to safety" attached to it. I think it's an idea that's pervasive in our culture and demonstrates a disconnection from our ingredients. As kids or beginner cooks, unless it comes out of a wrapper, we can hardly distinguish between foods that require cooking to be safe and those that don't.

This gap has made for a culture of overcooking. Why do so many people have terrible memories of vegetables? Because they were cooked to death. We were introduced to many vegetables like they were under-seasoned, mushy penance for something we did wrong. At some point, someone cooks them well and we taste the bright, fresh flavors with a crunch that's just right, and it's as if we've never tasted them before.

This tracks back to the pasta story, because it's our own anxiety that make us think cooking longer is better. It's a lack of trust in our ingredients and our palate that make us rely too much on timers, or think "better safe than sorry" while the flavor, and in some cases nutrition, in our food leeches out and evaporates before our very eyes.

Vegetables should be washed, but once in the pan, taste them for doneness—it's about preference, not safety. Meats are a slightly different story, but the same theory applies: once you've reached a safe minimum temperature, which varies by the protein, use your senses to guide you and you'll make tastier food.

Fear does not make a good cook. Trust yourself and your ingredients make a good cook. Trusting yourself and your ingredients makes a good cook.

Cherry Cobbler

Summer fruit is vibrant and fresh. Raspberries, strawberries, and cherries awaken our palates with zing and fervor. Delicious fresh in the field while kneeling in dirt, they're also classics in the oven. Cobbler, crisps, and pies all play on the same theory. Browned bits against baked fruit tastes great. I love the biscuity breadiness of cobblers and pie crusts and their many pairing opportunities, but also enjoy the less structured crisps that are typically topped with oats, butter, and brown sugar.

You can complement the fruit or the crust of the cobbler I chose to include here; either is delicious. Fruit ales will energize the lively fruit character, while barleywines or dopplebocks will contrast tartness and play off the browned bits like they were born to be there.

These instructions are built for your oven, but this makes a wonderful campfire dessert, banking the Dutch oven in coals above and below. Feel free to make the components in advance, so all you have to do is pour them in the hot cast iron and crack open a beer while you let the magic happen.

Serves 6-8

Cobbler Batter

1 stick (1/2 cup) butter, melted

1 cup flour

1/2 cup sugar

2 teaspoon baking powder

Pinch of salt

3/4 cup milk

1 egg

Cherry Filling

4 cups fresh cherries (or thawed, if frozen)

1/4 cup sugar

1/4 cup maple syrup

1 tablespoon lemon juice (alternately, you can use the peach filling below for peach cobbler, or improvise as you see fit).

Peach Filling

4 cups sliced peaches

1/2 cup sugar

1 tablespoon lemon juice

1 teaspoon cinnamon

1/2 teaspoon nutmeg

Directions:

Preheat oven and cast iron Dutch oven to 400 degrees F.

Combine cherries, sugar, syrup, and lemon juice. In a separate bowl, mix flour, sugar, baking powder, and salt together. Whisk milk and egg into flour, forming a smooth batter.

Pour melted butter into hot Dutch oven, immediately following it with the batter. Top the batter with fruit mixture, and do not stir. Batter will rise through the fruit.

Bake 45 minutes to an hour, until top is golden brown.

Consider topping with a spoonful of heavy cream.

FRED RANT

Listen to Your Palate, Your Brain is a Liar.

I come into this rant knowing it's a living contradiction. Often, we measure things based on whether they meet our expectations or not. We limit experiences based on what we think we'll like. Our brains are risk-averse, so they keep us in the channels or lanes that include what we already know we like and direct us away from anything we're unsure about or expect to dislike.

I had the pleasure to judge a really interesting competition with the good people of Mondiale de la Bier in Montreal one year. They host the Greg Noonan Memorial MBier competition. They use twelve judges and start out by

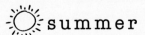

introducing and explaining the model and encouraging us to let go of any idea of normal and prepare to just taste. MBier is not only rated blind (an important criterion for any competition), but the judges are also blind to style. This means that I would get several beers in front of me per flight. They were various colors and came with nothing more than a four-digit glass code for record-keeping. In order to fill out our tasting notes and rate the beer, we were supposed to write down the style we thought the beer was and then judge by our own criteria for that style. I'm still amazed at how this changed my overall perspective.

For one, I can't knock a beer for being out of style, if I guessed the style. If I think it's more like a porter than a stout, I'd write porter. Visa versa, I'd write stout; then I'd get to judging.

It also completely changed how I tasted in the session, and affected my relationship with my palate forever. Without any information, and with several different colors and/or styles of beers per flight, I was starting my assessment and experience of the beer at ground zero. Knowing nothing, the first smell of the aroma was a gentle and sincere introduction as I began with no expectations. After several swirls and sniffs, I'd move on to that first introductory sip and let the beer slowly coat my palate and then dissipate. I'd quietly ask myself what I tasted, and would have to answer that by completely relying on my palate and nose.

The first day caused me some some anxiety, because I naturally worried about whether I got the style right or not. I asked if we would get confirmations of the styles at the end of the day or the end of the week, and they just smiled and said, "no."

To them, it didn't matter. They weren't awarding by style—they award the top ten beers based on their overall appeal to judges, not by style grouping or category. It didn't matter if I guessed it right or wrong; what mattered is that I tasted objectively and that naming the style was really for me. It did help organize my flavor memories as they came in, but it became less relevant and less worrisome as the hours and days passed. I felt my palate wake up, alive with interest because it was now identifying the first, if not all, flavors rather than my brain predicting things with expectations or even prejudices.

The contradiction is that it can be helpful to use our brains. Style names, beer descriptions, and beer dinner hosts all help set expectations of flavor that help you choose or prepare for something before you try it. I know that if I suggest a secondary flavor to someone during a tasting, they become more likely to taste it—usually a good thing. I set the expectation by mentioning it, and then the recognition is not only more likely, it's also typically more favorable.

I look at these moments as the brain working for "good, not evil." If it helps people understand a beer or a dish better or on a deeper level, it's good to feed our brain with information and expectation. I encourage you to taste blind as an experiment. This means you really don't know what's coming. Have a friend agree to bring things that you don't know are coming, across many styles and types, and just taste them. What do you taste? Do you like it? It's like palate calisthenics, and it's also incredibly freeing. I believe my open-mindedness and ability to identify flavors improved greatly during that week and has continued to grow since. I could practically hear my palate's sarcastic remark, "finally."

Autumn

autumn

Harvest

I had a pretty casual relationship with locally grown produce for a long time. I would nod in appreciation if a friend brought something from their garden, but I didn't think to arrange my eating around what was coming up or growing. I can recall a friend giving me a jar or two of "Grandma's pears," a sweet gift that didn't seem all that significant,because it wasn't filling a need. In fact, we'd have to find a way to make an occasion for them, so we didn't forget them in the pantry.

Driving the country roads of West Michigan, I would notice the roadside produce stands pop up with cardboard signs and drop-a-dollar coffee cans. Their tables would fill up with asparagus, cucumbers, and summer squash, all around the same time. It was cute, but it all seemed so momentary. I enjoyed the kitschyness of it all, but I didn't even think much more about it, and it certainly wasn't seen as a "need."

The grocery store had groceries; this roadside stuff just seemed like people's tasty little hobbies. The significance of not seeing the raising of food as a need points to our, or at least my own, disconnection, an occurrence I think is quite common today.

I began to value restaurants and chefs with a local or seasonal bent to them, simply because they were putting out the best food. As I ate their food, I was inspired by their cooking and also began to understand that they had a deeper philosophy behind how they wrote their menus. The fact that certain dishes might be on their menu for a matter of days or weeks, and then no longer available, seemed like a clever idea at first, a way to keep things interesting, rather than a sourcing reality. I smiled at Food Dance's decision not to use tomatoes on their burgers unless they were in season, not fully grasping the stand they were making against imported, modified, and therefore inferior tomatoes. People thought they were being dramatic, but later I realized they were refusing to put them on plates because they couldn't stand behind them. Over time, it became more clear to me. If you had a tomato at Food Dance, it was going to be delicious, because nothing less was tolerated.

By the time our neighbors joined us in putting in a relatively sizable garden, we were all pretty hip to the concept. We wanted to grow food for our kitchens. We'd eat what we could keep fresh and "put up" whatever was left for the Winter. As certain vegetables came on strong, we'd dig into the books and figure out the best way to store them. I made every zucchini dish I could muster that first season, as our plants were prolific. We froze, pickled, and canned, depending on what the book told us we should do, or what we remembered our grandmas did.

It was a fun project, but several moments sank in over the course of that first year and really shed light on our overall relationship with food overall. I was responsible for "processing," and there were moments when we watched the brightness of beautiful produce fade and then disappear because it wasn't processed in time. There was a sense of sadness or solemnness connected to that waste, although it varied based on how robustly or sparingly something grew.

Neighbors Matt and Amy had suggested that we would love using canned tomatoes all Winter long. "They're great to add into sauces and all sorts of things." I wouldn't call myself skeptical, but I wondered about it, because I hadn't found myself using many canned tomatoes up until then, unless a specific recipe like barbecue sauce or maybe a redsauce called for it.

As Winter rolled in, the opportunity to walk down to our freezer or canning shelves while we were buried during a snowstorm and eat the food that had grown ten yards away was remarkable. I'm sure it was part conceptual novelty and part nutritional fortitude, but making a dish with our home-canned tomatoes seemed so revolutionary. It was nothing short of an epiphany. Things changed.

It started slowly at first but, little by little, these jars of Summer were making it into all sorts of dishes, like chili, pot roast, collard greens, and improvised pastas. By the end of the Winter, I was eyeballing our shelf of tomatoes, gauging how I would have to ration them out to make it to next season. Sure, I could find more tomatoes somewhere, but these represented a slice of last season that literally could not be replaced, because no more of these particular tomatoes existed.

Collards were another lightening rod for me. We grew several cooking greens: collards, kale, Swiss chard, and mibuna something-or-other. I enjoyed them all, but collards really hit the sweet spot. I like them at dinner as a side, as an accent in soups, stews, and pastas, and as a base alongside our tomatoes in my favorite farm breakfast, "Eggs in a Nest" (thanks to Barbara Kingsolver's, "Animal, Vegetable, Miracle").

We had a ton of greens, and we made a processing assembly line out on our back patio. We brought them in from the garden in big laundry baskets. We trimmed the collards, chopped 'em, and blanched 'em in boiling water in an outdoor turkey fryer. After a couple of minutes in the water, we drained them onto big beach towels and rolled them up to squeeze out remaining water. We put them in Ziploc vacuum bags, then pumped the air out with one of those things that look like a mini bike pump. It took all of an afternoon, and I think we did it twice that season. The massiveness of those heaping laundry baskets shrank incredibly to twenty or so quart-sized bags of collards by the time we were done. We divided them up and threw them in the freezer. The joy I felt pulling those out of the freezer and making hearty, healthy food in January is frankly hard to put into words. I did not realize I could get so excited about an ingredient, especially a vegetable.

What's interesting is that without even knowing it, my cooking and eating patterns were shifting. I was imagining those ingredients and then creating dishes around them. Gone were the days of thinking dish first and then hunting for ingredients, no matter what month it was. Gone were the days of trying to figure out how to use something up, or hide it in something. I was genuinely inspired by the wholesome goodness of these ingredients that we had figured out how to make last well beyond their season.

It's important to remember that you're not necessarily keeping the food in the same state as its fresh version. I find I cook with tomatoes in the Winter and eat sliced tomatoes when they're in season. Freshly picked raspberries and blueberries are incredible and transcendent. Their texture and springiness are different after the freezer, but their flavor remains intensely regional. I'm more likely to cook them or otherwise process them after the freezer, whereas I like to eat them raw and untouched in their fresh state. Adapting and building dishes around these flavorful frozen gems is much more rewarding to me, however, than eating the fresh versions that have been shipped across the continent and are available year-round in the store.

I find it ironic that the off-season is what really connected me to the seasons. It was "putting up food" that connected me to the role we play in creatively expanding our opportunities to eat superior ingredients. I could see throughout the Winter that this was not a hobby, that this was about sustenance. I felt connected to history, and imagined how important this was to the generations before us who were known for these skills. Our grandmothers and their grandmothers weren't putting putting up food because it was cute or en vogue. They were storing food to feed their families.

"You gotta make hay while the sun shines." It's this function and purpose that helped me connect to the entire food cycle throughout the year. I appreciate those moments when food is at it's freshest and also love to taste the arc of an ingredient throughout the year. Our neighbor up the road grows plums commercially, amongst many other fruits. One day, seeing his plywood sign with "PLUMS" spray-painted on it, propped up against a tractor,

I pulled in, and after a half hour of small talk, I left with a half bushel. Another charming example of the social shopping experience. I went home and ate a couple, while wondering what the hell I was going to do with this many plums. After a little thought, I decided on a barbecue sauce made with our smoked rye dopplebock, Charkoota Rye. I had a whole-hog beer dinner on the horizon, and it would make a lovely addition. I went to work, digging into the canning books, and made a sauce that combined a traditional sauce and a plum chutney, as well as some of my own barbecue tricks. I canned them according to the guidebook and was delighted with the result.

The following season, I wanted to make it again. I dropped in on Gary and we talked plums. He advised that they were at their best towards the end of the season, at their most ripe. Then, he came up with a more "technical" answer, that I should come by "When I start thinking about taking the sign down."

I caught him late season, but when I got into the kitchen, I struggled to get the sauce right. I tweaked and tweaked, adding acid and really working to get the plum character I wanted. It took me a while to figure it out, but I deducted that late-season plums are great to eat fresh, but early season plums are brighter and less sweet, and just better for the sauce I like to make. I share this story because I learned that the art of putting up food allows me to capture that particular week in a plum's life in all of its glory. Even though I liked the first year's sauce better, I found myself grinning with this newfound knowledge and appreciation.

Before you skip out on me because you didn't buy this book on beer to learn about gardening, I want to share how the plum story takes us to the next point. You don't have to be a gardener to connect and capture the season's flavor and nutrition. The thrust of our garden's output pushed me into my own personal discovery, but what I love is taking that knowledge and applying it to the farmers market, or other situations like my neighbor's momentary plum stand.

Honestly, we have trouble keeping up with a garden. It's a ton of work, and we have busy lives. With canning and freezing on your side, though, you can leave the weeding to the professionals and capture the peak produce moments by buying the things you want to put up in bulk and going to work. What's more, you even get a little scheduling flexibility. You'll have a few weeks or more to choose from, depending on the ingredient, so you can buy it on a week you have time to put it up, whereas a garden has no mercy or appreciation for your busy schedule.

Buying in bulk makes you a slightly different customer at the farmers markets and stands, too. If you're going to can the tomatoes, for instance, you don't need the pretty ones that are all "graded" for market. Taking a lesson from several of my bulk food mentors, I learned to ask for "splits" or "seconds" on the days that I'm buying to put them up. If they have 'em, they'll sell you bushels full of produce that is blemished in some way, typically at a much lower price. It's still totally delicious for the canning cellar or freezer, so you're now preventing waste, spending less, and stocking up your cellar to keep your kitchen in local produce year round. Pretty cool stuff.

This responsibility also seems to tie me into the seasonal rhythm. There are weeks of happy-go-lucky, fresh food shopping and eating, but others where my Spidey Sense starts tingling and I recognize that the end is near for one ingredient or another; if I want it beyond its season, the time to store it is now.

This could all seem like more hassle than you need. I mean, isn't this what the grocery store is for? To some degree, that's true, and I'll tell you, our house is certainly not sustained completely by our own food storage. However, if you start with one or two things, ingredients you love and see a difference between the grocery store version and your locally found treasure, it will all start to come clear. We make plenty of exceptions, and

I'm grateful for quality grocery stores that keep us from being totally dependent on our cellars, but I have found the art of putting up food to be eye-opening and fulfilling in more ways than I can describe.

Better Than Correct

FRED RANT

My high school music teacher used to spend a great deal of time and effort trying to get us to understand a simple concept. We learned to play the notes and rhythms of the music on our instruments, and there was a certain relief when it all came together and everyone was playing the right notes. Mr. Patterson would respond to that relief with a sardonic challenge: "Congratulations, you just got to zero." It would usually cause a fair amount of frustration amongst my band-mates. You could feel kids rolling their eyes, thinking, "I played it right, what more does he want?"

It may have taken me a minute to grasp it as well, but this lesson I learned through music carries into just about everything I do, especially cooking. Doing things correctly is essential and has great value.

Whether it's playing the right notes, having enough yeast in your bread, or cooking meat to the right temperature, correctness has its place. However, it doesn't address the intangibles. Phrasing and expression give music something beyond the right notes. We know it when we hear it, that shift from mechanical to soulful. Some find this sooner than others, but we can't really access it until we get to correct, and then past it. Being correct equals zero. You've made it to the halfway point of being interesting—now what?

In the kitchen, this comes down to moving past the recipes and food preparation skills and into a deeper connection with your senses and palate. It's taste and touch and layering flavors, creating experiences that feel less technically impressive because their technique doesn't show through the graceful arcs and curves of flavor and comfort.

This is when and where food becomes our own. You can recognize a cook's food from these artful signatures more than you can from any specific ingredient choice. Their connection and aspiration to go beyond zero are what make the difference. Sometimes it's not adding anything at all, just as an artist knows when he's done, when he can't take anything else away.

Putting Up Food:
Resources

I don't want to scare you away from putting up food, but a little fear goes a long way with food preservation. While the techniques are simple, it is important that their functional properties are employed. You are preserving food, which means you're not only trying to save it for quality's sake, you're also protecting it from contamination, so sanitary procedures and food science are involved. Techniques and processing times change based on the type of ingredient and their acidity levels.

Think of it's you would baking—an occasion to use measuring tools, timers, and recipes—or shit doesn't work right. I'm not the one to teach you those things, but there are countless resources, and I refer to them often.

Some great examples follow:

"Putting Food By"

—Greene, Hertzberg, Vaughan

"Ball Complete Book of Home Preserving"

—Kingry, Devine

"Keeping Food Fresh"

—Aubertt

Eating Fall

"The best is yet to come, and babe, won't it be fine?"
—Frank Sinatra (Carolyn Leigh)
"As God as my witness, I thought turkeys could fly."
—Less Nessman

I love the diversity of Fall. It is the time of harvest. We've been eating fresh Summer foods for months, but Fall is something different. There's an amazing abundance of foods, as late harvest Summer vegetables like tomatoes and sweet corn are in their prime, while fruits like pears and apples complement the bright yet cool Fall days. Root vegetables and hearty cooking greens start coming in strong, robust fuel to prepare us for the cold days ahead. We're cooking outdoors, we're cooking indoors, eating fresh, and putting up food. The bright, crisp bite of a fresh apple is just as welcome as warm and comforting applesauce.

Similarly, we welcome robust beers as well as we enjoy the bright, fresh sips of Summer. With cool nights and warm days, all are welcome in our glass. I enjoy the abundance and seasonality of beers that play with fruit, herbs, and spices, like pumpkin ales and fruit beers. I also look forward to the earthy and engaging harvest ales, and the cozy comfort of browns and other malt-forward beers

Brewer's Garden Soup

We're not only harvesting food this time of year—it's also the time of year we're bringing hops in from the field. The Brewers Garden Soup is a nod to harvest ales, as it introduces hops via spirit that was steeped in hops. To me, it's a feel-good soup that captures that momentary sense of harvest, tying the earthy, herbal notes of beets and basil to fresh, aromatic harvest ales.

Brewer's Garden Soup

Serves 4-6

1 cup pearl barley

3 quarts vegetable stock, divided (homemade if possible)

4-5 beets

3-4 tablespoon olive oil (divided)

1 medium onion, chopped

1 medium fennel bulb, shaved or shredded

1 1/2-2 oz. Hatter Royale (dry-hopped white whiskey - alternately, steep hops in white whiskey or white rum)

1 1/2 cups chopped basil

1/2 pound fresh chevre (goat's milk cheese)

Kosher salt

White pepper, ground

Add barley to 3 cups stock; bring to a boil. Reduce heat to low, cover and simmer for 45 minutes or until done.

Toss beets in oil, wrap in foil, and roast in a pre-heated 375-degree F oven for 45 minutes to 1 hour. When done, peel off the skins with a towel and shred the beets in a food processor.

In a 4-6-quart soup-pot, sweat chopped onions in olive oil over medium to high heat for 3-5 minutes, seasoning liberally with kosher salt. Add shaved fennel, tossing to coat with oil. After a minute or so, add 1 1/2 oz. of Hatter Royale, stirring to integrate. (The aroma will develop almost instantly.) Add the shaved, roasted beets and chopped basil. Stir in 6 cups of hot veggie stock. Reduce heat and simmer for 15-20 minutes.

Add 1 tablespoon chevre, 1 1/2 tablespoon white pepper, and a couple pinches of kosher salt. Blend the soup with a stick blender for 3-5 minutes to desired consistency. Correct seasoning to taste.

Place an ice cream scoop-sized portion of the cooked barley in each bowl and ladle soup around it. Spoon "dots" of chevre into the soup and top the barley with a fresh basil leaf. Serve hot alongside a delicious glass of harvest ale.

Serves 2-4

Marinade

1/2 cup soy sauce

3 oz. sesame oil

1/4 cup fish sauce

4 teaspoon chopped minced ginger

4 teaspoon chopped fresh garlic

2 teaspoon ground coriander

1 teaspoon red pepper flakes

1 whole chicken, broken down for grilling

Peanut Sauce (2 chickens worth)

1 1/2 oz. unsweetened coconut milk

1/2 ounce lime juice

1/2 ounce soy sauce

1/2 tablespoon fish sauce

1/2 tablespoon hot sauce

1 tablespoon chopped garlic

1/2 tablespoon chopped ginger

3/4 cups creamy peanut butter

1/2 cup Ichabod Pumpkin Ale

2 tablespoon chopped cilantro

Greens

1/4 cup sesame oil

3 cups chopped collard greens

1 medium onion, halved and sliced

4 cloves garlic

1/2 oz. soy sauce

2 teaspoon hot sauce

1 tablespoon flax or sesame seed

Marinade

In a medium bowl, combine the soy, oil, fish sauce, ginger, garlic, coriander, and pepper flakes. Add the chicken and toss to coat. Let marinate in the refrigerator for 2 hours, turning occasionally.

Remove chicken from marinade and grill on a preheated grill 15-25 minutes total, starting bone-side down and turning halfway through, until internal temp of 165 degrees F.

Peanut Sauce: Combine the coconut milk, lime juice, soy sauce, fish sauce, chopped garlic, and ginger in the food processor. Add 1/4 cup of the beer and peanut butter and pulse. Add remaining stock until you reach the desired sauce consistency. Fold in cilantro, cover and refrigerate. Bring to room temperature to serve.

Greens: Heat sesame oil in a skillet or wok. Add sliced onion, top with soy sauce and hot sauce; sauté until tender, 3-5 minutes. Add garlic and toss; top immediately with chopped greens, tossing again. After 10 minutes, toss with flax seed, and correct seasoning to taste with soy and hot sauce. Check for doneness at 15-20 minutes.

Plate: Mound cooked greens on plate, top with chicken, and drizzle with peanut sauce. Add a ramekin of sauce on the side and serve with a cold glass of Ichabod Pumpkin Ale.

Ichabod's Chicken

Ichabod's Chicken was inspired by our pumpkin ale, Ichabod. The spices and pumpkin combine to create a very autumnal feeling. This is a pairing example that illustrates the strength of conjuring flavor memories and following your gut. In 2004, the first time I sipped Ichabod, my palate certainly shifted into culinary mode, as the cinnamon and nutmeg stepped forward. I'd be hard pressed to give you any technical reasons why, but shortly after my first sip, I was thinking about pairing it with peanut sauce. A few days later, I managed to give it a try and was thrilled, both with the flavor and that my palate had come up with such an independent and delicious idea.

This began as a chicken satay, but as I grew accustomed to buying fresh chickens from Eaters Guild, one of our local farms, I was inspired to use the whole bird, and adapted the dish slightly from there. I think its an exciting pairing and have won many bets against people who tell me there's no way a pumpkin ale will go with a Thai peanut sauce. I encourage you to do the same.

autumn

Dinner Party

You've gathered by now that I like to host people, and this includes hosting dinner parties. I embrace this time to join with friends, indulge in an unhurried meal, and kick back, enjoying each others company as well as bountiful food and drink.

We've covered a big part of the hosting angle, so I want to spend some time on structure and execution. I continue to learn and get inspired to shake things up and, consequently, the shape of my dinners is always evolving. There are so many ways to entertain over dinner that I thought it would be helpful to explore some options, especially as relates to artfully integrating beer to enhance the whole experience.

First things first. I want you to release yourself from routine. The fact that it's a dinner party means you can shake it up a bit and not cook, plate, or serve drinks the way you do on a normal night at home. This doesn't mean it has to be complicated or fancy; you just have room to creatively shape the experience.

The most significant shift I've made for the better over the years is to slow things down. Entertaining is about providing pleasure, not getting it over with. So many of our cultural habits have sped up over the years that we tend to naturally fight this idea every step of the way. We serve everything at the same time and we eat too fast, which is why when good hosts provide a pace that's luxuriously relaxed, people find it calming and enjoyable, even when they don't know why.

I'd like to explore a few elements that make up the various types of dinner parties you might have. Please remember, this isn't a textbook, it's a galactic guide, so these suggestions should be improvised upon, merged, tweaked, and riffed on. Your night is what you make of it. Put on your party hat and entertain!

Coursing your Meals: Most people associate the word "coursed" with a meal that is fancy or complex. Being treated to a "five course meal" conjures regal images of splendor and excess. I suppose that's true sometimes, but I want you to consider replacing all of those thoughts or images with words like "relaxed," "paced," or even "unrushed" or "well-phrased." I started out thinking I'd be describing the two types of dinner parties, coursed and uncoursed, but the reality is, I feel like I'm always building in some degree of coursing. It's just notalways overt. Let me explain.

Coursing is simply the act of serving parts of the meal separate from one another. If you have a salad first, followed by the rest of your meal, you essentially had a coursed meal; your first course was salad and your second course was your main course. This not only allows us some functional shifts, like different plates or bowls for different dishes, but to me, it also allows for some phrasing or graceful arc to develop over the meal. There are times to keep it simple and just sit down and eat your meal in one shot. I don't think of these occasions as unpleasant, I just think of them as less social meals. For me, lunch and weeknight dinners at home are my examples: they tend to be perfectly nice, often delicious meals, but I am looking for less story and a somewhat efficient timeline for the experience. Let it be known that while I strive for efficiency in my kitchen, I want my dinner guests, upon reflecting on their experience, to describe it as anything but "efficient."

So, if I've made the case for serving courses, what does that mean? It could be as simple as having appetizers out when guests arrive, followed by a salad and then the main course, which may still have a few parts to it, like steak, potatoes, and sautéed greens. If you think of this as courses one, two, and three, you can plan your time in the kitchen and serving accordingly. This means your main dish does not need to be done at a precise time, it just needs to come to the table at the right time. You gain more flexibility, because your guests are eating, drinking, and having a good time; timing should be on the cook's mind and no one else's. You'll need to plan what gets cooked ahead of time and what can happen between courses but, in general, stretching it out not only creates an enjoyable experience for the guests, but it lessens the amount you have to deliver at one specific moment.

Simple courses also allow for casual introduction of pairings. It's easy to shift what drinks are suggested or most easily available to the guests between courses. If you'd like one or a couple of beers featured with appetizers, have them chilled and out, readily available as people arrive. To shift to the next beer for salad, it's as simple as bringing them out from hiding and making them available. You can let the transition happen gradually and casually and be part of the overall composition, which some people will adjust to quicker than others, but the key is that you have opportunities for them to choose beers that complement the flavor arc of your dinner, because you created some broad-stroke phases.

Serving courses will take more time, which you may need to account for in your planning or communication. It can affect preparation, start times, and invitations. There is an art to finding the right amount of time, so people aren't feeling like it's dragging on. I love to create the feeling that we're taking our time and it doesn't have to all happen at once. When you're able to strike that chord, it resonates with people and makes them feel good—and that's why we're making them dinner.

Family Style or Plated? It may seem odd, but I ask this question about both food and drink. You have choices to make in terms of how to bring it all to the table, and it may change from course to course. The somewhat general and maybe obvious idea behind family style is that you're bringing platters of food to the table that will need to be passed or served. Plating is composing a plate per person, then delivering each one to the table individually. Of course there are advantages to both, and my decisions tend to be based on the dish, the size of the group, and even the occasion.

Family style is nice for one reason: it let's you shift things into courses without creating a ton of plating. If you think about a family style salad being passed around, you're able to slow things down at the table without slowing down the kitchen. There are also dishes that you really would like to keep hot as long as humanly possible, and keeping them whole, or en masse, is one way to do that. I have enjoyed bringing family style service to several public event dinners, because it warms the whole experience up for the guests while it speeds and simplifies service for the staff. Restaurants are not set up to serve every guest at one time, which is what large beer dinners require. If they have to drop one platter per four people instead of one plate per person, the food will stay hot longer and they can move on to beverage service that much quicker. It's also a good icebreaker in the restaurant setting to emulate home a little bit, and it gets people talking and sharing as they pass the pork.

Serving beer family style has some similar connotations, and surprisingly, we seem to overlook this option a fair amount. Something about beer and our history with it has us attached to serving size expectations. We tend to expect a full beer and/or the bottle it came from, right next to our glass. I love to take a page from wine's book and deliver bottles for the table. I like the community of sharing. I want people to be able to pour however much they'd like, a full glass or just a sip. If there is more than one type of beer at the table, I might like to have a little of each, and passing bottles around the table family style accommodates all of those choices nicely. The idea of having several different beers at the table does not mean you have to abandon your pairing post, either. I like to choose a few beers that will work; sometimes they're from the same flavor family, perhaps with subtle style or intensity shifts. Other times, I might be coming at a pairing from two or more different directions that can all be successful. Providing compatible choices is part of pairing well. It's not about exact science or controlling what and when people drink things together. I find this to be how I like to eat and drink, as well as a pleasant way to use your expertise without making a dinner with friends feel like a lesson or class. I like my guests to have room to share, sip, and discuss what they're drinking.

Plating: Plating is really about composing a dish visually, and it happens both on a family style platter as well as an individual plate. There's something personal about creating a plate for each guest that I enjoy. I don't know—maybe it's a bit like delivering a thoughtful gift, pleasantly wrapped for each person. It's funny; I really don't like one style over another, but after taking the moment to consider both, I typically feel strongly connected to the method I chose for a particular dish, a particular time. Plating can add complexity; however, with a little help it's easy to overcome. Having a stack of plates in the kitchen and a second person to bring them to the table after you compose each one can be pretty swift and efficient. Plating leaves the larger, full dishes in the kitchen and keeps them off the dinner table, which is nice spatially. It also means the table of people are not spending the time passing dishes and portioning their food, so when the plates arrive, you can sit down, raise your glass, and wish all present a hearty Bon Appetit!

There is a certain elegance in plated meals, and this goes for beer service as well. If family style is bringing the home into the restaurant, plating and drink service is bringing the sophistication of restaurant fine dining into your home. It's not about whether it's necessary; it's really a choice of style or even drama. Imagine if on cue, fresh glasses arrive, and over each guest's shoulder someone pours a beer intended for the next course. While, or shortly after, the glasses of beer are poured, plates are gracefully delivered in the same manner. The din of conversation will hush to a quiet hum. Guests will look at their food, each other, and eventually the host. A quiet, dramatic point has been made; your next course has arrived and you're going to enjoy the shit out of it.

I enjoy creating these dramatic moments when they're called for or available. It is important not to force them into situations where they don't belong. As your group increases in size, you need partners in crime to pull off moves like this. You need them in the game before dinner, so during the big moment you're not trying to explain what you'd like to have happen. Your conspirators simply roll into action.

Plating does not have to be that complex, however. It's often a simple consideration as I envision the dish taking shape. I ask myself what would serve it better and go with my gut for the answer. It is important to remember that this decision is really item-by-item, as the entire dinner is not dependent on one style. For instance, you might plate the main course, while also having platters of bread or gravy boats of sauce. It seems simple, but it's a good example that in some circumstances we're already making these decisions. We just may not have thought about all the places we can play, adjust, and improvise.

I might have family style pairings going on throughout dinner, but a very specific idea for one course. I want to shift gears gracefully, so the table will respond without feeling commandeered. "Plating" a glass service is one way to do that. Say you pour separate glasses of wheatwine in the kitchen, which are to be served with your favorite dessert. When it is delivered alongside dessert, it's really felt as part of that overall composed course. It should feel natural and easy, as no one has to finish their previous glass of whatever to enjoy it. For that matter, they don't have to indulge in the pairing at all; if they choose not to drink it, it's a glass of beer next to their plate that someone else will likely drink. By making it part of the course, I avoid the distracting moments of asking people if they want it or waiting for them to finish something.

This is all about phrasing and choices. I draw on the creativity that has always inspired me in my other pursuits, like music and writing. Create an arc to your meals by not only considering what you'd like to eat and drink, but how you're going to serve these components of the meals.. Your choices are sometimes simple things that can really personalize the experience for your guests. They not only feel your interpretation and your gift of hospitality, but they also experience a personal story of the dinner that is all their own.

Drunken Beer Belly

I created Drunken Beer Belly as part of a whole hog dinner set in October. The pear slaw brings those crisp fall bites while also drawing the fruity aspect of pork forward in a succulent manner. It's a versatile dish to pair to, because there's a lot to love with tripels, fruit beers, and other medium-bodied beers with subtle fruit.

Drunken Smoke-Braised Beer Belly

Serves 2-4

Serve this pork belly over generous portions of Drunken Raisin Slaw and pair with Envious.

2-4 servings of pork belly, cured or uncured

1 1/2 cups Black Tulip Tripel

1 1/2 cups apple cider

Place pork belly in a cast iron skillet. Combine cider and tripel in skillet (liquid should half-cover the meat). Bring to a simmer and transfer to smoker preheated to 225 degrees F (or preheated oven); braise for 60-90 minutes, until 145-150 degrees F. Rest before serving

Drunken Slaw

1/4 cup raisins

1/2 cup Black Tulip Tripel

1 tablespoon stone-ground mustard

2 tablespoon malt vinegar (or cider vinegar)

1 teaspoon lemon juice

1 tablespoon honey

Salt and pepper to taste

1-2 medium pears, peeled and thinly sliced into matchsticks

3-4 dried figs, minced

1 medium bulb fennel, shaved thin and sliced

1/4 cup cilantro, chopped

Soak raisins in 1 cup Black Tulip Tripel (or Envious) one hour or until hydrated; drain.

Whisk together mustard, vinegar, lemon juice, and honey; finish with salt and pepper to taste. Add pears, figs, fennel, cilantro, and drained raisins; toss to coat.

Deviled Scotch Eggs

Everything in moderation, including moderation. I preach keeping it simple, but every once in a while it's OK to make something because you can. I was inspired by a late-night introduction to smoked, pickled eggs in an undisclosed location. Ever since then, I've been developing variations of smoked deviled eggs, and wouldn't you know, they were even better wrapped in sausage. Subtle smokiness ties it all together and makes for a wonderful pairing with brown and Abbey ales. You can skip the smoke and start with hard-boiled eggs and still have a delightful appetizer. A variety of beers work well here; I enjoy browns, ambers, and IPAs.

Serves 6-8

6 eggs (a week or two old or more will peel better)

1-2 cups cider vinegar

1 lb. breakfast pork sausage

2 cups bread crumbs

1 quart vegetable oil (for frying)

2 tablespoon mayonnaise

1 teaspoon stoneground mustard

Pinch of salt

1/4 cup Freddy's Magic Rib Rub (from Boilermaker's Ribs, page 104)

Soak whole eggs in cider vinegar for 1 hour. Place eggs in smoker at 225 degrees F. In an hour, gently tap shells to form cracks to let more smoke in. You should see the white forming. Smoke for a half hour or more, checking one egg before removing the rest. Peel eggs and set aside.

Roll sausage into a thin, flat layer and divide into sixths. Hold in the palm of your hand, place egg in center, and wrap sausage around it, molding to close gaps. Repeat for each egg. Roll each sausage-wrapped egg in bread crumbs to cover.

Heat oil to 320 degrees F and fry eggs in oil 7-10 minutes until golden brown. Set on rack over paper towel to cool for 10-15 minutes.

Halve the eggs carefully and gently remove yolks to a bowl. Add mayonnaise, mustard, and salt to yolks, and mix well with fork. Load into piping bag or plastic bag with a corner cut off. Pipe yolks into center of the whites, and dust with rib rub.

NOBODY'S PERFECT

Deep Fried Distraction

Like most American males, I was attracted by the idea of deep-frying a turkey. You get to combine the burly experience of buying equipment at the hardware store with outdoor cooking and life-threatening danger. A recipe for perfection. There are many benefits to the technique: crispy skin, tender meat, and shorter cooking times.

When I combined deep-fried turkey with the big meal, Thanksgiving, I uncovered a few challenges I didn't see coming. I prepped a nice area on the back patio to do the frying and tried to follow the guidelines that would keep me from burning my garage down, like filling the pot with the turkey and water first to measure how much oil I would need.

There was a moment of reckoning, though, when I realized what I'd done to myself. On the biggest food occasion of the year, I'd added an extra cooking area outside of my kitchen. I had a dozen or so dishes to make and was constantly leaving the kitchen, disrupting my process and putting myself behind. On top of that, there are all sorts of horror stories that have created the not-so-subtle warnings with these fryers, that you should never leave them unattended. Perfect. Unless I figure something out, I have to monitor this fryer while my deserted kitchen gets further and further behind.

Of course, at this point I realize I need help, so I recruit my brother Greg for the job. "Hey man, can you hang out here and watch this turkey for me?" It seemed pretty simple to me, and Greg's a good sport, so I suppose it was. I realized, sometime later, the flaws in my plan (or lack thereof).

Recruiting guests to help is good practice, but asking someone in their nice Thanksgiving clothes to ride herd over a boiling cauldron of oil and poultry is not the best match. Not to mention, what does "watch this turkey" really mean? I think I had him watching the gas dial so we maintained proper temperature, but did I really expect him to jump in the mix and wrestle the oil rig if something went wrong?

In the end, we had tasty fried turkey and did not burn the garage down. I learned to look a bit further out and try to see when and where I would need help. If you think you're going to need some down-and-dirty help, give your intended assistants a heads-up. That way, they can get into the mindset and come with the idea of being true collaborators, rather then just getting pulled into emergencies

 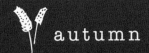

Drinking Fall

Malt: Brown Ales, Dubbles, and Barleywines

Brown ales and Abbey ales have a lot in common with the amber ale family of beers. They include caramel-like flavors, but tend to be a little more complex. Browns typically include a slight nutty character with pleasant roast, maybe even hints of coffee, but are generally very low in bitterness. There are a lot of variations on this, and brewers may use other grains like rye to accent their malt profile.

Belgian style dubbels and Abbey ales are also nice showcases for rich, malt character. They are balanced by subtle fruit characteristics from their fermentation, which provides nice support and structure to their slightly sweet and smooth body.

Barleywines and their cousin wheatwines are big, strong beers that are the best showcase for the caramel character found in beer. They are usually up over 9% alcohol, and they bring a booziness to their flavor that's part of their charm. Lying underneath the caramel are usually complex yet mingled flavors of fruit, figs, or raisins. These are warming beers, both in body and alcohol. Don't be afraid to let them come up to a slight chill, as their personality and depth will show through at warmer temperatures.

While there's a range of strength and intensity in these styles, they all make dynamic pairings. They're also excellent beers as ingredients in sauces, stews, and soups, as their sweetness and roastiness are terrific additions and don't tend to read as very bitter. The bigger the beer, the more likely there is bitterness lurking in the wings, quietly doing its job in creating balance. It's possible this bitterness can come forward as you cook, so be gentle, use butter, and taste often.

Hops: Harvest Ales

Harvest ale is a historic style of beer that showcases brewing's agricultural roots. Brewed in early fall, it is loosely defined by style parameters and more defined by philosophy. In harvest ales, brewers showcase their locales with a notable ingredient, hops. Contrary to the IPA, Double, and Imperial IPA trend, harvest ales present the aromatic and herbal components within hop-forward beers, balanced with malt flavors.

Brewing with fresh hops captures flavors only available at harvest time. My best food analogy is fresh basil. I make pesto, put it in the freezer, and love it year-round. I'll happily use dried basil in sauces and other dishes eight months of the year, but fresh basil has its own character, its own moment in time, and dishes like Insalata Caprese that celebrate the herb exclusively. Harvest ales, available for a brief but glorious moment in time, capture fresh hops in a similar light.

The most traditional way to use hops is to dry them first. This intensifies the character of the hops and provides an efficient way to handle them in the brewhouse. Think of the large handful of fresh basil you'd use in cook- ing versus a tablespoon of dried. Wet-hopping, a technique common to harvest ales, uses undried hops fresh from the field. This process varies from brewer to brewer, but consistently brings forward earthy, vegetal, and herbaceous character in addition to hops' more well-known bitterness and floral aroma.

Harvest ales have unique profiles and personalities, so pair to food with your palate rather then any standard rule. Most often, I think of these flavors as I would herbs and imagine what a good companion would be. Where do we like herbs? For me, roasted poultry, salads, fresh garden salsas, and fresh-veggie soups all come to mind as delightful companions to a harvest ale. If I headed towards pork, beef, or lamb, I'd incorporate a more herbal approach to the meat to bridge back to the beer. A marinade of basil, garlic, harvest ale, and lemon would hook a loin, steak, or chop up with a harvest ale right-quick.

Cellar: Dubbels, Tripels

Tripels share a lot in common with other Belgian-born farmhouse ales. They often use candy sugar to add fuel for fermentation, creating slightly stronger golden ale with bright, bready maltiness, with distinct fruit and spice from fermentation.

Tripels can lean towards pepper, but often present banana and other fruits like apricot or apple as part of their profile. They are outstanding with desserts, especially baked goods with fruit, and they are a secret weapon with pork. They also tend to bring forward new and exciting flavors when paired against ginger.

Wood and Fruit: Pumpkin Beers

Pumpkin beers punctuate a season when our palate craves and embraces the feeling of Fall. They share with fruit beers a sometimes-deserved reputation as being a gimmicky add-on to beer. We'd miss out on some really tasty beers and excellent flavor bridges, however, if we let an inaccurate stereotype keep us from the charming seasonal character of a good pumpkin beer.

Pumpkin ales are often a variation on an amber ale, with pumpkin and spices added. The ratio between these two is really where the beauty and preference lives. One person may want a heavily spiced pumpkin ale; another is looking for more subtlety. They are all out there, so this is a really fun style to do tasting parties or sessions with, tasting though eight to ten different interpretations with friends.

You can bridge to pull out the pumpkin, or use the spices to accent your food. Their flavors do well in both savory and sweet situations, so they can be served throughout dinner or at dessert.

Glassware

SOMEWHAT TECHINICAL

The shape and style of the glass affects the entire flavor experience, especially the aroma. Your glass also affects temperature and effervescence, and they can create flavor shifts as well.

Go to an advanced "beer bar," especially one that focuses on Belgian-style beers, and you'll see shelves and shelves of different types of beer glasses. Volumes have been written about which style goes in which glass, and there are many people who can give you a list of rules on how to avoid doing it wrong.

That's where I beg to differ. I'm on board with shape being important to flavor and style, but I don't subscribe to the theory that choosing glassware needs to be complicated, intimidating, or chastising. I've had beer taste pretty damn good out of an enamel coffee cup, so it can't be all that hard and fast.

I once heard a Belgian importer speak regarding the practice of each brewery requiring their beer to be poured in the brewery's proprietary glass, each of which had a unique shape as well as brewery logo logo. He was addressing a room full of professionals, and he continued by explaining that this was not a marketing gimmick or branding shtick—it was a centuries old tradition. I recall laughing out loud, thinking, "So, doesn't that make it branding shtick that's a couple of centuries old?"

Notice there are two parts that are indelibly merged. The shape of the glass is changing, which does have an affect, but by requiring a different logo and thus shape for every beer, it has gone well past what's necessary or even reasonable. I'm a branding romantic as much as anybody, so I'm perfectly content to be served beers this way by conscientious, skilled beer and glassware experts. It's just important to know that you don't have to.

The shape of the glass will impact how the aroma is delivered. If the bulb or bottom of the glass is wider than the mouth or top, the aroma, carried by the CO_2 that is departing the beer through the head, is pointed more directly towards your sniffer. If the mouth is wider than the bottom, it is less focused, thus the CO_2 is still leaving and still carrying aroma, but it's a softer feel, as it's not pointed straight at your nostrils.

Beervangelist's Three Glasses

The Tulip Glass: This is my desert island glass. I find any and all beers are enjoyable in this glass, especially the big, round, and complex beers that are associated with it. A stem keeps the bulb off the bar, making a gradual temperature change more likely. If you want to warm it up, you can cup it in your palms; if you don't, you just leave it alone. This style is commonly used for Belgian-style beers like saisons and tripels as well as other strong beers like barleywines or Imperial stout.

The Pilsner Glass: A Pilsner glasses is typically straighter-walled, with a base that's smaller than its mouth. These are great for bright lagers and a few ales like kölsch. Of course, kölsch-style beers have their own glass too, but I find a nice pilsner option will cover your needs for this whole range.

The Pint: The pint glass has a lot of history with beer. It's the only glass so ubiquitous in size. There are many shapes, styles, and even sizes, and we warmly refer to the idea of "meeting for a few pints."

This is somewhat of the universal glass for average-strength and common styles. Pales, IPAs, amber ales, brown ales—all the way down the line. I prefer a pint with some shape to it and thinner walls. I'm completely over the straight-walled shaker pint you see in so many bars. They feel thick and clumsy to me, and offer very little enhancement. They were made for shaking cocktails, and that's where they belong.

Before you go read your bartender the riot act, there are reasons pint glasses are the bar owner's friends. They stack well and are thick enough that they don't break easily, so I don't see them going away in the near future., But you can always ask for a glass you'd prefer over the pint..

Size: Apparently it's part of getting old, but my preference for glass size keeps getting smaller. I like glasses in the ten-to-twelve-ounce range. Whether I'm looking to try something else, or just sticking with what I'm drinking, I like having the opportunity to taste in smaller quantities. I enjoy pints as well, but if you have good service, you just don't need giant beers.

The way I look at it, which is not very scientific, is that all other glasses are variations on these three basic shapes. The snifter is an extreme tulip glass, while the small vertical kölsch glass is like a piccolo pilsner glass. A goblet could be interpreted by experience as a pint glass on a stem, with its wide walls and wide mouth.

Glassware makes a difference. You'd be well served to consider it as you set up your bar or kitchen at home. Find your favorite for each one of these three purposes and you'll have a nice set on hand for whatever beers your friends bring through the door..

Salt and Pepper

Seasoning is the most important concept for any cook to understand. Unfortunately, it is also challenging for emerging cooks to grasp, whether they're at home or in professional kitchens. Under-seasoned food is such a let-down, mostly because it's just such a waste of potential, but also because it is ultimately boring.

Salt is the workhorse of the two, and the biggest game changer. Salt's role with food changes throughout the process of preparation and is crucial at every step. The biggest mistake people make is a conceptual one. It's very easy and frustrating to see when someone holds the belief that salt goes on food rather than in it. I can think of a couple of very specific and tasty exceptions, where I want the sensation of direct contact with salt, but the beauty lives in engaging it early, often, and with purpose.

Salt is like the Underground Railroad. It's a component in rubs, marinades, and brines because it carries flavors inward, slipping past borders and breaking down barriers. It also helps break flavors out. A well-seasoned steak is seasoned well before it hits the grill, and you can see the exchange in process while it coaxes flavors out, moistening and maximizing on potential. Salting eggplant in advance extracts moisture and reduces bitterness.

Sweating onions involves sautéing assertively salted onions, cooking off the water, and making them tender and flavorful. This same idea is true for mushrooms and mirepoix, a combination of onions, carrots and celery which is a base for countless dishes and sauces. People often pull up here because they're afraid to make their food too salty, but they are missing the point. Salting early in the process is all about function, not flavor. You're not going to taste this salt—you're going to taste the way it worked with heat and fat to make those onions a deliciously sweet ingredient for whatever they're going into.

I also consider salt the brightener, which means we're not trying to taste the salt itself or change the flavor context. This is described simply and eloquently in a beautiful and inspiring cookbook, The Cooks House, by my friends Eric and Jen: "When you salt, what you're looking for is a lack of flatness."

Pepper has a slightly different role, as it's primarily flavor related, but it also benefits from being put to work throughout the process, building layers of flavor rather than sitting on top. Layering pepper gives it a chance to be beautifully ambiguous, linking arm and arm with the rest of the dish and/or its beverage companions. Whether it's aggressive or subtle, pepper is the supporting actor, and is well served by joining the cast through in appearances.

Table-side salt and pepper are good for a few things, like hardboiled eggs, freshly sliced tomatoes, and maybe adjusting the seasoning of fries. Other than that, I hardly use them, mostly because it's too late.

 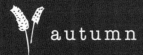

Pork Chops and Applesauce

I didn't truly understand applesauce until I made it. It is incredibly simple, but when you make it in season from fresh apples and serve it warm as a side, it will change your opinion of applesauce forever. Fall is traditionally when the family pigs are harvested, and we keep up the tradition. Pork chops are what I cook first, and they are also decidedly simple to make. Tender and delicious, pork chops and applesauce are a classic, and wonderful with their Belgain-born counterparts, Abbeys, dubbels, and tripels. If you have thick chops, finish them in the oven instead of braising, or overcooking on the stove.

Serves 2-4

2-4 pork chops

1 cup fennel rub (See page 181)

4-6 medium sized apples

2 tablespoon butter

1/4 cup turbinado sugar

1 teaspoon cinnamon

1 teaspoon lemon juice, more to taste

Rub pork chops in fennel rub, featured in Beer Brined Turkey and let stand at room temperature while you make applesauce.

Place apples in saucepan and add just enough water to barely cover. Bring to a simmer and cook for 30 minutes or more, stirring occasionally, until they begin to disintegrate. Add butter and continue to stir, mashing as you go. If you desire a smooth consistency, blend with a stick blender. Add sugar, butter, and cinnamon; stir and taste. Finish with 1 teaspoon of lemon juice. Taste and adjust lemon or sugar.

Preheat oven to 350 degrees F. Heat an oiled cast iron skillet on the stove to medium-high and add pork chops. Sear both sides. If chops are sufficiently browned yet not cooked through, move skillet to oven to finish. Bring chops to 140 degrees F and rest on a board 10-15 minutes as they finish to 145 degrees F.

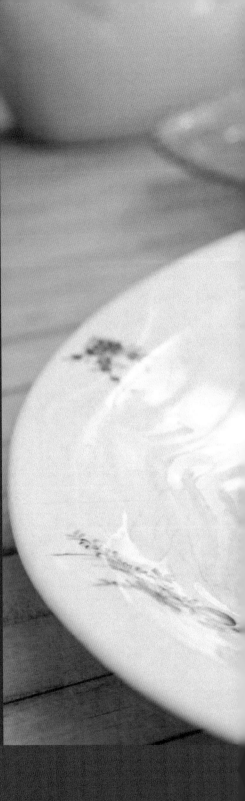

The Potluck

I swear I have PPSD—Post-Potluck Stress Disorder. "Bring a dish to pass" used to give me the heebie-jeebies. I've grown to appreciate these events, however, so I'd like to share how to productively participate in what I now see as a delightful community engagement. Of course, if you're nothing like me and find all potlucks perfectly enjoyable, you can skip over my ravings or hopefully still pluck a few new ideas from this diatribe.

Let me start by describing what I didn't like about potlucks. As a cook and an entertainer, I felt they involved a loss of control. I didn't have confidence that my guests would bring appropriate dishes, or that they'd be timed well, or even that they would be good. I think the biggest fear was that people would bring duplicates, and we'd have a table full of variations on potatoes au gratin.

I also found it hard to time things. I was always shooting to have all of my pieces coming together at just the right time so everything would be hot and headed to the table at the stroke of dinner time. When you insert someone else and their dish into that mix, it's a bit of a crapshoot. They're traveling from somewhere, so they would likely need to warm it up or even cook the whole dish, and that would mean that I'd have to coordinate my kitchen or oven with the whole thing. The few potlucks that I succumbed to usually had some sort of discomfort attached to them, from someone unknowingly committing one of my potluck sins.

I'm sure you're thinking that one of the solutions to this problem is for me to lighten the hell up, and that is true to a certain degree. After learning my own lesson, that "It's not about me," hosting or attending a potluck certainly became easier. I stand committed to PPSD prevention, and so I offer the following lessons and suggestions.

Don't require a "Dish to Pass." The first problem with this idea is that by including "Bring a Dish to Pass" on an invitation, you're essentially committing everyone, or at least every couple, to a dish. This can apply pressure and create fear for people who don't cook, and it will also almost invariably create an overabundance of food. It's almost impossible to have any sort of balance between food types, like hot and cold, or starch, vegetable, and protein. If you have hot dishes, can you keep them hot? The list goes on.

Collaborative Menu vs. "Pot Luck." I learned to take "luck" out of the equation by reaching out in advance and talking with the guests involved to figure out who should bring what. I might start with a question, inviting those interested in contributing a dish to suggest what they want to cook or prepare. From there, I can select and revise, creating a menu with balance from the options presented. Since they volunteered, I'm less likely to get someone out of their comfort zone, because they will most likely only suggest things they're good at.

If three people suggest salad, I can reassign two of them to something else. When you have a menu figured out, you can talk about prep and what people need. Ask if they want to join you in the kitchen, or are they bringing it ready to go? For instance, if they need a half hour in a 375 degree oven, you'll be much more able to make

Cabin Fever Carbonade

Serves 4-8

Beef stew meat (1-2 lbs.)

Flour

2 parsnips

2 turnips

1 medium-sized yellow onion

15+ pearl onions

1-2 cups chopped carrots

1-2 cups Shitake/Portobello mushrooms

6 cups beef broth

Fresh rosemary, thyme, Herbs de Provence

2-4 twelve oz. bottles of brown ale (Cabin Fever)

1-2 cups chopped figs

1 tablespoon brown sugar

4 Bosc pears, as crisp as possible, peeled and sliced into chunks

Salt and pepper, to taste

Toss beef in flour. In stew pot, sauté yellow onion and mushrooms, season with salt and pepper. In separate pan, brown beef at high heat. Add browned beef to onions. Add pearl onions in with beef to brown a little. Add broth to pot to cover as you go. Deglaze beef pan with beer and add to pot. Add carrots, turnips, parsnips, and figs to pot. Season stew with rosemary, thyme, bay leaf, and Herbes de Provence. Bring to simmer, cover, and simmer for 1 1/2 hours total. Dust peeled pears with brown sugar and sauté at high heat to brown. Set aside and add to stew a half hour before serving.

Cabin Fever Carbonade

Carbonade is a Belgian-style beef stew that puts all of these Fall flavors together. Slow cooking owes its life to onions, carrots, and other root vegetables, flavorful companions to beef which slowly break down into tender morsels, all part of a flannel-shirt-wearing kind of stew. It'll warm you up and stick to your ribs while still keeping an elevated, elegant feel.

it happen if you see it coming, rather than being surprised. There is also a great opportunity to turn this into a group-cook sort of potluck, where your friends might be preparing part or all of their dish in your kitchen. I love cooking with other people, and shifting into "helper" or sous chef mode in support of a friend is a great opportunity to welcome new ideas and learn a few new tricks.

Shoot the gaps. By hearing from your guests first, you can see where the holes are and plan your contributions accordingly. This doesn't mean you have to start the conversation with nothing, just don't commit yourself until you know what you have coming. For instance, we recently celebrated my wife's birthday with a potluck dinner in the neighborhood. She requested an Asian-style dinner, so that's where we started. The email went out, people volunteered dishes, and I built a menu from there, assigning myself the courses that remained.

Trading courses. Another great tip is that we essentially split courses rather than dishes within a course. Giving someone a course let's them direct traffic in the kitchen and on the table for that course, which, if nothing else, provides a little clarity. The time between courses is pleasant for the guests, but it also makes it easy for the kitchen to switch gears, shifting who is in the kitchen and what pans are on the stove at any given time.

I have had fun in the past creating a dinner where five of us drew courses from a hat and each had to bring the course with an appropriate beer pairing. I also recall a fun dinner for which each person was to build a course centered around a single ingredient, in this case, rhubarb. It was big fun, and also delicious.

What can I bring? Whether you're in a full-blown potluck or not, people often want to contribute to the evening in some manner. For some, it's more than a casual desire, as it is often a matter of upbringing. Their parents and their parent's parents raised them with the belief that showing up at a dinner without something to offer the host is nothing short of rude. I bring this up because it helps me consider their perspective when deciding how I'll answer the question, "What can I bring?" I may think I'm being hospitable and generous by insisting that they not bring something when I may actually be creating stress. Over the years, I've learned to adapt my answers and genuinely think about what someone can bring, allowing them the pleasure of contributing. If we're in potluck mode, this heads down a menu path, and I may consider what gaps are left and whether they are asking to cook or just pick something up? Beverages & fresh bread are items that can be picked up without too much hassle, and are generally welcome at any dinner, no matter how much you may have already. It's also an opportunity to riff on pairings by asking several guests to bring their own favorites within a given style, or perhaps their own suggested pairing for a certain dish.

Outside the box: As a cook, I tend to get a little tunnel vision on the food and drink, especially when collaborating. There's great fun in engaging your friends in the other parts of the party as well. Think about suggesting fresh flowers, or asking someone to volunteer to set the table. Some people leap at the chance for an opportunity to have fun with decor, and it's typically much livelier with a little outside energy. I think my favorite contribution beyond food and drink of recent note was inviting our friend Heather to DJ the Asian Birthday Party. She came packin' with a killer playlist, hooked into the kitchen stereo, and guided the dinner party through hours of remarkable ambience. It eventually devolved into a remarkably memorable chocolate fondue dance party. It's an example of something I completely appreciated but would have never gotten to if I did it all myself, and she was thrilled to dig in.

By coordinating and communicating around potlucks, you're able to direct the arc of your dinners, engage in pleasant collaboration, and give everyone the opportunity to contribute from their place of comfort. You'll be part of the PPSD-prevention team, and you'll give yourself an opportunity to discover the joy of adding a kitchen DJ to the mix.

Thanksgiving

I could call this section "Holiday Dinners" to be more inclusive, but Thanksgiving and I have such a history together that I feel it might be insulted if I don't give it proper attention. I'm from a big family, and I've been hosting Thanksgiving for about fifteen years, so many of the hospitality lessons I've learned have either come from Thanksgiving or been tested at it.

For most Americans, this November Thursday is the Holy Grail of holiday dinners. It is the holiday when the family meal isn't part of the tradition, it IS the tradition. I truly do love Thanksgiving for that. However, it presents a unique set of challenges for the hosts—let's just say it is the Holy Grail of challenges, too. The menu is traditional to the point of being iconic; stray too far from the classics and you risk upsetting history and/or a family member or two. There are more dishes packed into this menu than any other meal we eat... just about ever. I mean seriously, it's roasted turkey, a dish most people don't get a lot of practice at, with about a dozen sides, most of which are expected to be served hot. It's a lot to manage for even the experienced cook.

You have to juggle all of these culinary challenges amidst a kitchen and house full of guests, a solid dose of family pressure, tons of distractions, and maybe even some intense emotions as you cook for your friends and family and hope for the best.

I love Thanksgiving. I think all of those challenges add up to it being the Grand Prix of Holiday Dinners, because it's like a street race: you're tackling high speed, expert-level challenges on roads built for normal traffic. Your kitchen isn't designed for this many dishes to hit the table at once, nor is your dining room.

To me, while the Thanksgiving meal remains the ultimate challenge to cook, it's also a master class on hospitality, on being a good host. It is where I learned so many of the valuable lessons I share with you in this book. I have a Thanksgiving story of failure and success for just about each and every point made in "The Habits of a Good Host." I don't regret any of it, but there are definitely two sides to the coin. I learned how to cook my way out of deep trouble, mostly because I was really good at getting myself into it.

As much as I've bitched about the pressure of traditions, I must say my family is very flexible. I've arranged the menu many different ways. I've smoked, deep fried, deconstructed, and beer brined the turkey. We've had the meal plated and coursed, family style and buffet, with and without beer pairings. I've included potluck conspirators, sous chef friends, and niece and nephew prep cooks. Over time, I have learned to engage more people and drive more towards the experience I wanted my guests and myself to have, which is to relax and enjoy the time together.

I realized through all of these years that I couldn't provide that feeling to my guests until I found it in myself and in my kitchen. As the menu became more comfortable for me and I was more "off book," not relying on recipes, I started to shoot for different targets, and things started to relax. I imagine, and I think my family would agree, that all of the dinners were good, but they started to warm up in an altogether different way when I was able so share more calmness by shifting some things around, honoring the experience more than any one dish.

Thanksgiving still has the mother of all "crunch times," so there will always be some intense moments, but a looser grip and proper planning can set you on a course that will reduce stress and improve the flavor of everything.

I'm going to share a style of dinner service not described in "Dinner Party" because it's typically only pulled out for big events such as Thanksgiving, and that's the buffet. There are all sorts of connotations, many of them negative, with buffet. I believe it's mostly because of the food some people choose to serve at them, or the context they're used to seeing them in. I want to break down why they can be great and how I got there.

It used to drive me crazy to go through the crazy gymnastics in the kitchen, to have hot food coming off the stove and out of the oven all at the right time, only to watch it get cold while seventeen people passed it around the table for twenty minutes. Finding a place for all of the platters was also a serious challenge, and once everything was passed, the food was scattered around the dining room, waiting to be served as cold seconds, shadows of their former selves.

So one year, I decided to plate Thanksgiving. I was going to take this thing upscale. I made a delicious soup course to start, followed by salad and then the main dishes of Thanksgiving. By coursing dinner, I could reduce the number of dishes being served at once, and plating would guarantee everything was being served hot and the way I wanted it. I even introduced pairings with each course. Well, it was a nice idea. I had recruited some help and had a pretty good plan for getting the plates, bowls, and glasses out of the kitchen and into the dining room. I had not accounted for all of the dishes that would be coming back to the kitchen during dinner, however, and that became a serious problem, as I was simply unprepared to receive them. This plan also meant I needed to be cooking throughout the entire meal. I could stop by and say hello, sit and grab a bite, but I always had to get back to the kitchen to prepare the next course, amongst my towering stacks of dishes from the last one. Great idea but, like I said, our kitchen and dining room weren't built for it, and my family actually came over to hang out with me a little bit, rather than just wave to the guy in the kitchen.

From there, I discovered the value of chafing dishes and the buffet line. For the un-indoctrinated, these are essentially portable racks with steaming water in pans that hold trays of food above the steam. With a lid, food can stay warm for hours. It is not ideal for all foods, but the comfort foods of Thanksgiving actually does pretty well with it, as they "hold well." It took me a minute to realize how much this could shift my preparation. The first year, I still had most of the food coming up right at dinnertime, so the challenge of getting it all out to the chafers was still pretty intense. Over time, I realized which dishes held the best, and I could prepare them well ahead of time, freeing up the oven or stovetop earlier and leaving more room mentally and physically for the dishes that needed to be completed closer to service. Add the practice of resting the turkey a significant amount of time, like an hour or more, and the pace of the whole thing started to slow down.

The table was elegantly set, with certain passable items and accouterments, but the hot dishes hit the chafing pans, and once everything was assembled, we'd call guests to the table. I enjoyed the meal, talking and sharing with my family, and even enjoyed seconds, which were still warm. It was a new day.

I'm not done, however. I still have a bone to pick with Thanksgiving, my favorite of all holidays. I am inspired by my Danish in-laws and their penchant for all-day dinner parties, which I've been lucky enough to attend. It was at the end of one of these dinners, when I was euphoric after more than eight hours with countless courses of delectable food, brought out in what seemed to be the most leisurely manner, that I found myself proudly inviting the Danes to Thanksgiving, our foodiest of holidays. As I finished up describing the wonderment of Thanksgiving in all of its splendor, I realized we still have so much to learn. I feel like I found our culture's Thanksgiving flaw. Like an impatient teenager, we take all of this beauty, dish after dish of luxurious, autumnal comfort foods, and we pile it high on our plate and eat it all at once. In thirty minutes of glory, it's over.

This realization doesn't tarnish my love for the holiday, but it does challenge me to be an agent of change, while not making it about me, of course. I want indulgence to be about how much we bask in the unhurried meal with great company, a leisurely pace, and splendid flavors. I want to reshape our day and enjoy hours at the table, learning to rest ourselves as well or better than we rest our poultry. I have a plan, and it's surprisingly simple. This year, things are going to be different. With any luck, I'll tell you all about it in Beervangelist's Guide to the Holidays.

Beer Brined Turkey

I've hosted Thanksgiving for more years than I can count, and I've cooked turkey with many delicious techniques. This beer brined recipe is my favorite by far. IPAs bring in flavor, aromatics, and moisture. The beer helps avoid drying out any part of the bird and makes cooking time a considerably more relaxing process, especially after you've made it a time or two.

The fennel rub is optional, but I highly recommend it. It makes the most gloriously colored turkey, and the aroma in your kitchen will have your neighbors asking to join you for dinner. I also make stuffing separately, as an open cavity with lemons and herbs not only creates great flavor, it helps your turkey cook more evenly. It also allows me to adjust the batch size of the stuffing to my guests rather than my bird(s). Homemade stock with your stuffing recipe will more than make up for any flavor you might have gained from cooking it inside the turkey.

Serves 12-14 (1 1/2 lbs. per person).

Fennel Rub

1 cup fennel seeds

2 tablespoon white peppercorns

3 tablespoon kosher salt

2 tablespoon ground basil (dried)

Put the fennel seeds and peppercorns in a heavy pan over medium heat. Toss to toast evenly to a light brown color, being careful not to burn the seeds. Remove to plate and cool completely before grinding. Pour the seeds into a grinder and add the salt and ground basil. Blend to a fine powder, shaking the grinder occasionally to redistribute the seeds. Store in a tightly sealed glass jar in a cool, dry place or freeze.

Beer Brined Turkey (cont.)

Brine

1 cup kosher salt

1/2 cup light brown sugar

1 gallon vegetable stock

1 tablespoon black peppercorns

1/2 tablespoon allspice berries

1 tablespoon Fennel Rub

1 gallon (two growlers) Mad Hatter IPA

4-6 pounds ice

Combine all brine ingredients, except beer and ice, in a stockpot and bring to a boil. Stir to dissolve solids, then remove from heat, cool to room temperature, and refrigerate until thoroughly chilled. 6-12 hours before cooking is to begin, combine the brine and iced beer in a clean 5-gallon bucket or chest cooler. Place thawed turkey breast side-down in brine. Add beer or ice to cover bird, close cooler/cover bucket, and refrigerate or set in cool area (like a basement) for duration of brine (6-12 hours.) Turn turkey over once halfway through brining.

Turkey

1 large (18-21 lb.) whole turkey or two small (8-10 lb.)

Turkey Stock (or substitute 2 cups chicken stock)

2 small whole onions, peeled

2 carrots, halved

2 celery stalks, halved

1 quart chicken stock

1/2 cup extra-virgin olive oil, divided

1/2 cup fennel rub

8 sprigs of fresh herbs, any combination of rosemary, thyme, sage, and oregano

2 lemons, halved

3/4 cup all-purpose flour

3/4 cup butter

Place necks and giblets into a large saucepan. Add onions, 2 carrots, 2 celery stalks, and the chicken stock. Bring to a boil over high heat and then reduce the heat and let simmer until reduced to about 2 cups. Strain and reserve for gravy.

Turkey: Preheat the oven to 425 degrees F. Wash the turkey(s), inside and out, and dry well. Coat inside and out with half of the olive oil. Season each turkey on the outside generously with the fennel rub. Insert herb sprigs and 2 lemon halves inside the cavity of each turkey.

Set oiled and rubbed turkeys onto roasting rack and pan. Drizzle remaining olive oil over bird. Roast until an instant-read thermometer (inserted deep into the thigh but away from the bone) reads 165 degrees F and juices in the thigh run clear when pierced with a fork, about 2 to 2 1/2 hours. Remove from the pans and let rest a half hour to an hour, before carving. Reserve pan juices for gravy.

While turkeys are resting, make the gravy. In a medium-heavy sauce-pan, cook 1/4 cup flour and 4 table-spoons butter over medium heat for 3-4 minutes, or until a blond roux is formed. Add pan juices and home-made turkey stock (alt: chicken stock) and bring to a boil over high heat. Reduce the heat and let sim-mer until thickened and ready to serve.

To Brine or Not to Brine?

Brining is a technique that is incredibly useful for roasting meats, especially poultry. It often comes up around Thanksgiving. I imagine it seems like kitchen voodoo, which can be a little intimidating to the uninitiated.

The way to remove the shock and awe is to understand the role of brining and a little bit of its science. A brine is a liquid with a high concentration of salt, created by dissolving salt into it. The salt desires equilibrium, so when meat is soaked in a brine, the salted liquid penetrates the membranes through osmosis and heads inward, attempting to balance the amount of salt inside with the amount on the outside. The fact that salt's vehicle to the interior is liquid means we didn't only send salt inside, we send moisture as well, the primary purpose of brining.

This technique is a valuable in many situations, but is best with either whole roasts like chickens and turkeys or skin-on roasts. The skin prevents you from leeching other flavors out of the roast while you send your liquid magic in. The bigger the roast, the more time you should allow for the process to take place.

Sugar is also added to most brines, typically at 1/4 to 1/2 the amount of salt, although the ratio varies all the way up to equal parts. To me, the best way to understand the idea behind beer brining is that as long as you're sending liquid in, it may as well contribute flavor. You can create different flavors by adding herbs and spices and by substituting other liquids like beer and stock. I like to avoid a straight beer brine and often go half beer, half stock. I want the benefit of the many favorable attributes of beer, but I don't want to be so overt that it tastes like a beer-stuffed chicken. Remember, your roast is going to be on heat for a while, so evaporation will be taking place, and we want to keep balanced flavors in check.

I think it's a great opportunity to cook with aromatic and herbal beers from the hopcentric family. They complement other herbs in the brine, and the evaporation will be less than other applications, so their aromatics tend to stay intact as pleasant contributions.

The benefits of brine are many. For poultry, you're roasting for long periods of time and have different needs for various parts of the bird. When cooking to get the dark meat to temperature, oftentimes the breasts and white meat will become dry. Additionally, there is a tendency to overcook poultry, as cooks want to avoid serving any undercooked poultry, which is a food safety issue. Brined birds will have a much longer "cushion" past the first minutes or degrees of being done before they become dry. You can cook past your targets to be safe and still have tender, moist chicken throughout the entire bird. It's like magic, and not only tastes great but will give the grillmaster some sweet relief from the stress of grilling chicken for a crowd

Thanksgiving Smoker

I was twenty-five or so when I first offered to cook Thanksgiving dinner for my family. That first year, I took over cooking at my parents' house, after which I got brave and invited them to my apartment.

It was somewhat of a coming of age experience to invite my family over for a big holiday dinner, and I wanted to make it special. I had been hearing a lot about smokers and smoking food and, at some point, I heard about smoking a whole turkey. "Now that sounds cool!"

After reading my first book on smoking, "Smoke & Spice," the hook was set. "Any chump can roast a turkey for their family; I'm going to smoke one." Of course, this requires that you own a smoker, which I did not. So, in mid-November, a week or so before the big day, I started the search—which involved the Internet, phone books, and a lot of calls to area stores. I hadn't bargained for this hunt, because all of these stores said they carried them, so why don't they have them in stock? I seemed to be as out of touch with seasonal equipment as I was with seasonal food.

After much haranguing, I found a store that said they had one in their seasonal trailer, and if I made it out there, they'd dig it out and sell it to me. Jackpot! I made the arrangements and brought home a Brinkman electric smoker the day before Thanksgiving. I was all set.

Well, I uncovered a second problem, which was that I couldn't find anyone with the bags of wood chips you use for these things. Stores were closing for the holiday, and I was striking out. Without chips, I had a heating element under a turkey, which is remarkably close to roasting, and we've already determined that's for chumps.

I'm not one for giving up on a project, so I relayed my troubles to my increasingly concerned girlfriend Ulla, who was already managing the other aspects of our dinner that were clearly beyond me, like table settings and other essential items. Turned out, Ulla had logs of applewood at her apartment, which I decided were perfect for the job. A quick run to her place and I was one step away from firing up the new smoker—I just needed to turn the log into chips.

So there I was, sitting in my enclosed porch/office, hacking away at a log with a screwdriver at 11:00 pm, hoping to get the smoker started by midnight so it could smoke the recommended fourteen plus hours. Relaxing story, ain't it?

Even though I managed to get the turkey smoked, and I'm sure I did OK on the other dishes, this is not an all-star memory. I was so focused on a fancy technique and the show that I wanted to put on that I completely overlooked the original objective of simply hosting my family for a holiday dinner. The other details from that year have faded, because all I can remember is the frenzy of my smoked obsession. I am quite certain that my hosting efforts would be described as neither relaxed nor gracious, and that I delivered undue stress and chaos to my hosting partner.

I'm also quite certain that a simple, well-executed, roasted turkey would have tasted delicious. Remember who you're cooking for and be willing to give up on an idea for the greater comfort of your guests.

Don't Rush the Rest

I imagine most of you have heard about "resting" roasts and poultry. It's the idea or technique of letting the roasted protein sit for a bit once pulled from the oven so that, as it cools, the juice retreats back toward the center. This way, when you slice it, instead of the juice running out onto your cutting board and drying out the meat, it stays in, making for a moist and tasty morsel.

I'm amazed at how many times I have caught myself "rushing the rest." It's a contradiction at it's best, and it's all user error. Oftentimes, I would calculate my roasting time, add a little bit for the rest, and work backwards from dinnertime to decide when to start cooking. Reliably, the roast—especially if it's poultry—would take longer than I imagined, which eliminated any time to rest. My side dishes would be done and hot, the guests would be seated, and I'd be standing at the oven, thinking about what pairs well with impatience.

At that point, it's pretty hard to let your chicken rest, so you're destined to cut into it early, because everybody's waiting on it. I had to ask myself why I was doing this. I figured it was most likely my desire to serve food hot—but then I challenge myself by asking, how hot do we really want roasted poultry? I have never heard anyone rave, "Man... that chicken was piping hot!" That didn't stop me from trying to time it to the minute, however, and I'd get burned every time.

I've grown to embrace the fact that we actually appreciate roasts at warm temperatures, not hot. Left whole to rest, it will take them a long time to dip below a pleasant serving temperature. You can rest from half the amount of time you've roasted to equal the time and have a very pleasant experience. This means chickens might rest forty-five minutes to an hour and a half, turkeys twice that amount. This time frees you up to be more restful and relaxed as a host, too. When guests arrive, the house smells of herb-roasted loveliness, a whole bird is on the board, resting in all of its golden-brown deliciousness, and life is good. It's the savory version of the comforting homemade pie cooling in the window.

You can leisurely share a beverage, a story or two, or even finish up your side dishes at a relaxed pace. Carving should be the last thing you do, and it is so much more pleasant for you and your guests when you can carve it gracefully, actually touching the meat without scalding your fingers. Serving up some hot gravy or sauce from the stove can address any longing you have for a little heat or steam from your plate.

Resting is so much more than a technique; it's really a way of life. So learn from my errors and don't rush the rest.

Pear Tart

This Danish tart with Envious poached pears is inspired by my mother-in-law, Inga. It is a delicious dessert that one need not have a sweet tooth to enjoy. Gorgeous alongside triples and fruit beers.

Serves 6-8

Poached Pears:

4 ripe Bosc or Anjou pears, peeled, halved, and cored.

1 quart beer (preferably a malt-forward style with underlying fruit)

1 quart water

2 lb. sugar

1 vanilla bean, split

1 cinnamon stick

10 black peppercorns

Place the sugar, beer, and water in a large pot and stir to dissolve the sugar. Add the vanilla bean, cinnamon stick, and peppercorns, then the pears and place a small plate over them to keep them submerged. Place over medium heat and bring to simmer. Poach gently until the pears are easily pierced with a paring knife. Cool the pears in the poaching liquid overnight. Remove from the liquid and pat dry.

Piecrust:

10 tablespoon chilled butter

1 cup all-purpose flour

1/2 cup sugar

1 teaspoon vanilla extract

1/2 teaspoon ground ginger

1 egg, beaten

Water, if needed

Cut the butter into the flour until incorporated, as if you were making a traditional piecrust. Add the egg, ginger, and vanilla extract and knead gently until fairly smooth, adding a little water to moisten if needed.

Divide the dough into two roughly similar pieces, flatten each into a disc, and refrigerate until well chilled and firm.

Roll each disc to 1/8-inch thickness and about 10 inches across. Use one to line the bottom of an 8-inch ceramic or glass pie tin. Lay the pears in the pie tin snugly, then top with the remaining dough, pushing it gently over the contours of the pears. Crimp the edges together, brush with a little water, and dust with coarse turbinado sugar.

Bake in a preheated, 395 degree F oven for about 40 minutes, or until the crust is set and golden brown. Remove and cool for about an hour. Cut one whole pear per serving and top with ice cream. Serve immediately with a dollop of crème fraîche.

Winter

Cellaring Beer

Cellaring beer is the act of storing beer for an ample amount of time to enjoy later. Much as with pairing, one should be aging beer with an expectation of change. It's a little counterintuitive, because the change you're hoping for is actually a slow degradation of the beer. I enjoy the process because it reminds me of us as people. We're all aging, which includes some wear and tear. In our younger years, the age hardly shows from one year to the next, but given enough time, you see the effect of time more prominently. We are drawn to people who age gracefully; we can feel their history through their eyes and read the character drawn in their face and hands. There are subtle parts of their charm that we can't describe; we just admire and want to be near them, appreciating what time and experience have created within them.

To me, vintage beer is very much the same. Beers that have aged well show a certain grace and charm. Beers that were once brash and bold often become nuanced and well-rounded. Complexity is usually shown through layers of subtlety and intrigue. Flavors are often indescribable, as they're a composite of craftsmanship, time, and experience.

It sounds romantic, and it is, but cellaring beer is also a risk. The reality is we are counting on age to take it's toll on these beers—we're just hoping we've selected beers with character that will age gracefully. Accepting this risk is a big part of enjoying a cellar program, as it will lessen the sting of discovering some of your precious cellar might not have made the journey. Tasty or not, consider it all a conversation or journey and take the good with the bad. This is a personal experience, because whether you like what you taste is the ultimate, and really only, assessment. Accordingly, there are no hard and fast rules here, just a few guidelines that will lessen risk and enhance your experiences.

Selecting for the cellar: Alcohol is a preservative and will contribute to a beer's ability to stand the test of time. Traditionally, people brewed low-alcohol beer as a method to extend the safe water supply. If you're looking to cellar beer for a couple of years or more, you'll want something a bit stronger. I consider 7.5% alcohol by volume to be the low watermark, although I've seen many exceptions work. Remember, we're looking for something more than just "holding up," so you'll want to look beyond just the ABV. I look for depth of character, beers that have richness, complexity, and maybe even a little edginess to them. Basically, you want to start with something that has enough body to develop and soften over time and still be present and interesting.

As time marches on, hops and hop aroma are typically the first victims. This doesn't mean you can't vintage Imperial or double IPAs, but it does mean their character will change faster than other styles. It also means that if your favorite part of a beer is the hoppy aroma, perhaps that's a beer you should drink fresh. These beers typically have big malt bills to balance their hops, which provides a richness to pick up the lead.

On the other hand, malt-forward styles like Russian Imperial Stouts, barleywines, wheatwines, and other strong ales are prime candidates. Their fresh assertiveness rounds and softens over time, providing lushness and depth. I also love Belgian tripels and sours. Their spice, fruit, and tartness become symphonies of nuance, blending intricate vignettes of flavor with every sip.

Buying for the cellar: The biggest piece of advice I have for buying beer for the cellar is to buy more than one of anything you're "putting up". In order to gauge how a beer is doing over time and whether you'd like to drink it now or save it, you have to taste it now and again. If you only have one, while it may feel special, it also increases your risk of regret, as you're opening a little more blind. You can mix up styles or pick a few favorites and buy bottles from each year so you have the opportunity to pour "vertical tastings," which is when several vintages of the same beer are tasted side by side.

Cellar conditions: Beer likes it cold and dark. Refrigeration is always the best-case scenario, but it's rarely an option for long-term storage in the home. Cellar temperature is perfectly fine; for these purposes, I would consider anything below 65 degrees F. Beer should be stored upright overall, but it's a must for unfiltered beers. When you're aging, you don't know whether filtered beers will encounter any sediment during storage, so use the same rule for all. This allows the sediment to stay on the bottom rather than in the shoulder, which means you can decant to serve and leave the sediment in the bottle, not in your glass.

Tasting from the cellar: There's a double-edged sword with beer cellars. You need to put the beer out of sight and out of mind so you don't drink your favorites in their first year. On the other hand, it's easy to overlook and forget to enjoy, which can lead to wasting beers that age past their best years from abandonment. I'm also a "take the toy out of the box" guy, so I am storing beer to drink, not to be some untouchable collection. Think about creating moments to taste, bringing a bottle up for a special dinner or inviting friends over for a vertical sampling. These are great bottles to share, sip, and discuss, enjoying the subjective experience and talking about what different people pick up in each beer. I'm much better at this at the brewery than I am at home, but it's a good idea to take some notes so you can see the story of a beer over the years, noticing what changed and when you thought it was at its best.

Eating Winter

Winter is the Olympics of comfort food. Around here, the fresh foods we can still source in this season are root vegetables, cooking greens, and hydroponics. With any luck you've got a cellar and freezer full of tasty supplies to take you though the winter. To me, a well-stocked cellar when the weather turns is more comforting than wool or flannel.

Even if you didn't put up food, it's a great time to take a few cues from the idea and cook as if you did. Our palates enjoy the restorative, soothing tones of hearty, rustic cooking. It's a time to dig into your roasts and practice your slow cooking.

Comfort food brings comfort beer, so bring on the sippers and big, warming beers. Winter is the time for robust character and depth of flavor. Sour ales or Imperial IPAs bring nice punctuation amidst many dark ales that I'm fond of in front of the warming glow of a wood burning stove.

Beervangelist Chili

The folklore of chili, more specifically, chili con carne, begins perhaps as early as the Incas, Mayans, and Aztecs, although the cowboys and trail hands of Texan cattle drives are presumed to have made the dish a legend. There's tell of a resourceful range cook planting herbs and spices along his route, picking and drying them on the side of his chuck-wagon his next time through.

Chili con carne is essentially "chilies with meat," and early Texas chili was likely not much more than trail-caught meat rubbed with salt, ground chilies, and spices simmered in water with onions and garlic over a slow campfire until tender "enough". As a horseman, I can imagine the efficiency of this, as the pantry ingredients would travel well and make a mean "bowl of red" after a long day in the saddle.

Traditionalists argue that "chili" has no beans or tomatoes, no way, now how. Others will allow them if identified, such as "chile con carne y frijoles," and even more don't consider it chili without beans. I'm a no-rules chili maker. I keep the history in mind, but beans and tomatoes are allowed. I'm inspired by my neighbor Fenn Valley Vineyards and Winery, whose only rule in their annual cook-off is that you enter in the appropriate category: four-legged, two-legged, or no-legged (think animal, not cook). Enjoy Beervangelist Chili with porters, stouts, and IPAs.

Serves 8-10

1 medium onion, finely chopped

8-10 garlic cloves, chopped

1 pound beef stew meat

1 pound ground bacon (or ground pork)

1 1/2 teaspoon kosher salt

12 oz. barrel-aged stout (or amber ale)

32 oz. tomatoes (home-canned if possible), ground or chopped

32 oz. canned black beans, drained

2 chipotle peppers canned in adobo sauce, chopped with 1 tablespoon of their sauce (to taste)

1 tablespoon chili powder (home-made is best: toast dried chilies, cool and grind)

1 teaspoon ground cumin

2 teaspoon black pepper

2 teaspoon dried oregano

Optional: 30 corn chips or 3/4 cup corn meal as thickener

Brown seasoned beef and bacon in saucepan or Dutch oven. Add onions, cooking until tender; add garlic and deglaze pan with beer, scraping browned bits off pan. Add remaining ingredients and simmer for 1-2 hours, stirring occasionally and covering after the first hour. Refrigerate, degrease, and reheat to serve.

Serves 4-8

Savory Crepes (make ahead of time)

2 large eggs

3/4 cup milk

1/4 cup water

1/4 cup oatmeal stout

1 cup flour

3 tablespoon melted butter (for batter)

1/4 teaspoon salt

Blend 7-10 seconds, rest refrigerated for 6-24 hours.

Melt additional butter in a crepe or omelet pan on medium heat. Pour enough batter in to just cover pan after rolling it round to spread batter. As bubbles form, flip until both sides are a toasty brown color and crepe is fully cooked. Set aside and repeat until all crepe batter is finished.

Duxelles

2 tablespoon butter

1 medium onion

1 lb. mushrooms of your choice, 1/2 diced, 1/2 sliced (avoid dense mushrooms like shitakes, and select some that will cook down well)

4 oz. milk

1 cup shredded Chihuahua cheese

Sweat onion in butter; add mushrooms and season with kosher salt. Reduce to 1/3 original mass. Add milk and simmer until reduced and sticky. Add cheese and stir, seasoning with salt and pepper.

The Build: On a sheet pan, layer duxelle between crepes, 6 or 7 high. Top with Parmesan cheese and tightly chopped chives. Warm at 250 degrees F. Cut into wedges and serve.

Crepe Duxelles

I've been cooking this dish for a long time, although I didn't make it up. It is the quintessential pairing example for mushrooms, inspired by the wonderfully talented mind of Alton Brown. Crepe Duxelles is delicious anytime, but especially tasty with the earthy mushrooms of late Fall and early Winter. Another nice thing about it is it's somewhat of a pantry meal, with the crepe made from flour, milk, and fresh eggs, which are always available with a little looking, even in the late months of growing season.

I think of this dish as rustic luxury. It reads French indulgence, but without being fancy. Richness from the dairy and the deep, earthy tones of the mushrooms are all layered figuratively and literally into a tasty, tasty bite. It'd be decadent by appearance only, but once you dig in, there's just something grounding about the simplicity of it all.

I love oatmeal stouts with this dish. Their roastiness is a familiar contrast to the rich dairy and a delightful complement to the dark and lovely sautéed mushrooms. Porters and other modest stouts would be wonderful as well, just be careful to keep them modest, as this pairing is all about comfort.

The Cook's Pantry

I have grown to realize the value of being prepared in your kitchen. Keeping a well-stocked pantry lets you react and respond to the fresh ingredients that find their way to you. I don't find myself shopping for these things based on dishes or recipes anymore; they're what I count on having on hand.

They will allow more creative freedom for you to concoct dishes by having more options available. They're also pretty handy for what we used to call "recessionary cooking," those moments when you don't want to leave the house and need to cook with what you have. I can make many a tasty meal from this pantry, whether I have fresh ingredients or not. This means they're especially important in the off-months, when there are fewer fresh ingredients available. Cooking from your pantry, freezer, and canning cellar is not only an enjoyable art, it'll save your ass if you get snowed in. As long as you don't run out of beer!

My Go-To Pantry Items:

Rice

Pearl Barley

Polenta

Pasta

Nuts (pinenuts, walnuts, almonds)

Peppers (dried, canned)

Dried mushrooms

Sundried tomatoes

Stock (homemade in freezer, store-bought in pantry)

Rubs (Freddy's BBQ, fennel)

Salt

Pepper

Sugars (turbinado, cane)

Flour

Bread yeast

Olive oil

Veggie or corn oil

Vinegars (rice, balsamic, sherry, cider, malt)

Coconut milk

Black beans

Home-canned tomatoes

Hot Sauce (Siracha)

Honey

Freezer:

Pork, beef, lamb

Stocks (various homemade)

Leftover bones, etc. (freezer packed to make stock from)

Fruit (raspberries, blueberries, cherries)

Corn

Greens (collards, kale)

Basil and pesto

 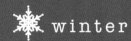

The Beer Dinner

 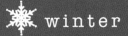

Fred Bueltmann

"Beer Dinner" is a term used to describe a coursed meal with established beer pairings. It's most often used by restaurants that are hosting a special dinner, selling seats in advance, and including the pairings as part of the package price. Of course, formats change from restaurant to restaurant, and there are many creative variations on the theme.

Beer dinners are a great chance to explore flavors, as chefs are usually creating dishes around the beers, and brewers are often present to talk about their beers. I find that chefs love to stretch their culinary legs and make food that is not on their existing menu. There's more freedom to explore ingredients and shake things up, and they don't really have the obligation to repeat it, so they can really cook in and for the moment.

Many dinners will be a collaboration with a single brewery for the night, so their beers will be featured. Other times, the restaurant may work with several, perhaps a brewery per course or any other combination they can dream up. I once collaborated on a dinner with another brewery where we each provided one beer per course, and the pièce de résistance was a literal blend of two beers, one from each of us. A pairing that really lived in that particular moment and did so beautifully.

Keys to Enjoying a Beer Dinner:

Taste the pairings, but don't feel you have to finish them. This seems simple, but I have seen people wave off the pairings without ever trying them, which always seems like a missed opportunity to me. These are the times that beer can and will surprise you. Open your mind and throw away any preconceived notions about beer or beer styles. On the other hand, the experience is about flavor, so feel free to sip and leave beer behind. Most experienced restaurants will be pouring reasonably sized samples designed to pace your meal, but occasionally I see full beers get delivered with each course. It's also OK to not like a pairing. The nice thing is, more often than not, there's another one coming.

Change it up. People ask me which is first, the food or the beer? It really is a chicken and egg question, and I encourage you to try both. Whichever you try first, think about what changes the next time around, after each exchanges flavors with the other. How did the food adapt to the pairing, and what did the beer taste like after the food, or on the third sip? Inviting questions will allow you to taste more aspects of the pairing and appreciate the shifts.

Give it time. Serving several courses with pairings to a large group is a pretty big undertaking, and it takes time. Expect these dinners to take a little longer, and plan accordingly. Whether or not it's all going according to plan, sit back, relax, and enjoy the pace of it all.

Show up. No, seriously, show up. Chefs are often bringing in special ingredients for these dinners, portioned for the exact number of seats. Last-minute cancellations are brutal and can really throw a curveball to the kitchen. I don't mean to nag, but it is not like a normal reservation. If you can't make it, get somebody else in the seat.

Hall of Fame

I have been inspired and grateful to participate in some wonderful beer dinners over the years. I often remark to the crowd that these evenings of intense flavor and pairing are a wonderfully indulgent experiences to be enjoyed. We should also borrow ideas from them that we can carry to any meal, any time. Each harmonious connection between ingredients or between food and drink that awakens something in our palate and creates higher expectations is a good moment. These dinners have changed how I think about flavor and have informed my process when making simpler choices, like what I want to drink with dinner tonight.

They have also inspired me to create deeper connections with food and ingredients, including starting a Harvest Dinner with the chefs and crew of Paul Kahan's Publican Restaurant in Chicago. We all headed out on a farm tour of Michigan farms. We tasted, talked with farmers, and sourced ingredients for a meal we'd make the following week. We created the menu and pairings during the trip and enjoyed our immersion and how far into the moment we were able to take our process.

This turned into an annual dinner and trip as well as similar harvest collaborations with the local and talented crew at Salt of the Earth, led by Chef Matthew Pietsch. In 2013, I will host six farm tours across our region, engaging food, beverage and farms in rewarding and flavorful conversation.

Here are some menus from beer dinners that have stuck with me and are part of my own personal highlight reel of collaborations, conversations, and flavor memories.

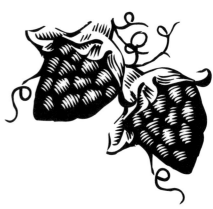

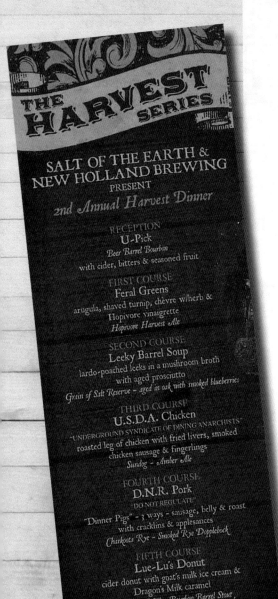

THE HARVEST SERIES

SALT OF THE EARTH & NEW HOLLAND BREWING
PRESENT
2nd Annual Harvest Dinner

RECEPTION
U-Pick
Beer Barrel Bourbon
with cider, bitters & seasoned fruit

FIRST COURSE
Feral Greens
arugula, shaved turnip, chèvre w/herb &
Hopivore vinaigrette
Hopivore Harvest Ale

SECOND COURSE
Leeky Barrel Soup
lardo-poached leeks in a mushroom broth
with aged proscutto
Grain of Salt Reserve - aged in oak with smoked blueberries

THIRD COURSE
U.S.D.A. Chicken
"UNDERGROUND SYNDICATE OF DINING ANARCHISTS"
roasted leg of chicken with fried livers, smoked
chicken sausage & fingerlings
Sundog - Amber Ale

FOURTH COURSE
D.N.R. Pork
"DO NOT REGULATE"
"Dinner Pigs" - 3 ways - sausage, belly & roast
with cracklins & applesauce
Charkoota Rye - Smoked Rye Dopplebock

FIFTH COURSE
Lue-Lu's Donut
cider donut with goat's milk ice cream &
Dragon's Milk caramel
Dragon's Milk - Bourbon Barrel Stout

The Publican & New Holland Brewing Co. Presents:

Taste of Michigan II
august 30, 2011

welcome
Farmhouse Hatter

salad
country ham & melon
arugula & radishes
. . .
Beerhive Tripel

poultry
roasted chicken
ground cherry salsa
. . .
El Mole Ocho

meat
grilled flank steak
peperonata
. . .
Dragons Milk

cheese
poet's tomme
tomato jam
. . .
Sundog Amber

dessert
sweet corn ice cream
coffee streusel & dark chocolate
. . .
Pilgrim Dole

The Publican would like to thank the
purveyors who contributed to this del

Eaters' Guild Farm - Bangor, Mic
Jake's Country Meats - Cassopolis, N
Seedling Farm - South Haven, Mi
EverGreen Lane Farm & Creamery - Fenn
Mick Klug Farm - St. Joseph, M
New Holland Brewery - Holland, I

$55/guest
optional beer pairing $15/gu
[not inclusive of tax or gratu

---

5 COURSE BEER DINNER
OCTOBER 27TH 2010

Happy Daze Cocktail w/ Hatter Royal
Curried mussel soup.

1ST COURSE
Envious
Shaved Allan Benton 2yr aged ham,
japanese pear, apple, pine nut watercress.

2ND COURSE
Golden Cap
Whole roasted American Red Snapper
with late harvest caponata.

3RD COURSE
Charkoota-rye
Young Earth Farm pork shoulder brined in cider, served
over braised cabbage and caraway mustard spaetzle.

4TH COURSE
Dragons Milk
Imperial Cat's Meow.
(Disco version of an FD classic)

5TH COURSE
Imperial Hatter
Artisan American Cheeses. Cow's milk selections.
Vivace Bambino— Cato Corners Farm
Caved Aged Cheddar— Blue Mont Dairy
Dolce Gorgonzola— Swiss valley Farms

Journeyman: Cicerone Dinner 2008—Chef Matt Millar
Beer Dinner with New Holland

RECEPTION

Parmesan gourgeres with Kathy Halinsky chevre & chive

Salt cod, garlic & Bintje potato fritters

Full Circle Kölsch

AT TABLE

Shellfish ragout with Boeve Farm leeks, lemon thyme, sweet cream, & frites

Golden Cap Saison

Pumpkin agnolotti in parmesan broth with pumpkin seeds, brown butter, sage, & Styrian pumpkin seed oil

Ichabod Pumpkin Ale

Blackberry glazed breast of smoked magret duck with braised lacinato kale, carmelized shallots, and duck liver & balsamic vinaigrette

Blue Sunday Sour Ale

DESSERT FLIGHT

Dulche de leche custard with muscavado caramel

Pilgrim's Dole Wheatwine

Tobacco chocolate truffle

Dragon's Milk Bourbon Barrel Stout

Black walnut & olive oil cake with fall berries & maple crème fraiche

Black Tulip Trippel

Goredawnzola blue cheese with Hasselman's honeycomb

Existential – Hopwine/Imperial IPA

Station 5
CHEESES/SALADS

Marinated Vegetables, Olives,
and Assorted Peppers

International and Domestic Cheeses

Fresh Sliced Seasonal Fruits

Chop Salad with an Assortment
of Vinaigrettes

Whitefish Pâté

Duck and Pistachio Pâté

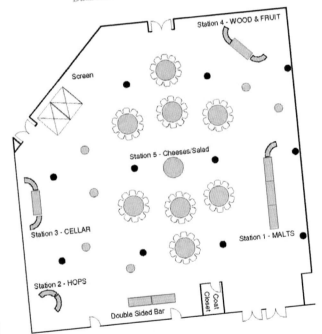

RECEPTION
Welcome to an evening of Beer & Food Pairings

Thursday, January 14th
in Kalamazoo 1

Michigan Brewers Guild and MBAA – District Michigan Winter Conference

January 14-15, 2010
Radisson Plaza Hotel – Kalamazoo Center
Kalamazoo, MI

Station 1
MALT-FORWARD

The beers at this station feature the many flavors of brewers' malt. From grain-powered spiciness, caramel sweetness to coffee-laden roastiness, these beers are paired with foods that capitalize on these rich flavor-bridges.

Arcadia Ales
Sky High Rye

The Livery
Telewhacker Brown Ale

Beer Bread Canapes with Rye Mustard and Rabbit Sausage and Rattlesnake Sausage

Dark Horse
Amber Ale

Dragonmead
Eric the Red

Fried Green Tomatoes with Goat Cheese and Gruyere

Keweenaw
Widowmaker Black

Wild Mushroom Ravioli with Roasted Tomato Sauce

New Holland
Charkoota Rye

Founders
Breakfast Stout

Cherry Buckle with Drizzled Chocolate Sauce

Station 2
HOP-CENTRIC

This station features beer with hops as a significant part of their signature. The foods selected play off the aromatic, floral character, notes of grapefruit and playful bitterness.

The Livery
Steep Canyon Pilsner

Founders
Red's Rye

Fried Beer Battered Walleye Slider with Pilsner Tarter Sauce

Dark Horse
Crooked Tree IPA

Saugatuck
Singapore IPA

Short's
Huma-lupa-licious

Build Your Own Lettuce Wraps: Jerk Chicken, Matchstick Carrots, Red Peppers and Bibb Lettuce

Bell's
Hopslam

Key-lime Shooters

Station 3
FROM THE CELLAR

These beers feature the flavors of fermentation. Yeast character, esters or other tastes of the cellar are prominent in the flavor profiles and the elements of the pairing.

Corner Brewery
Brasserie Blonde

Michigan Brewing
Celis White

Peppercorn Encrusted BLT with Sliced Tomato and Micro Basil

Jolly Pumpkin
Maracaibo Brown

Roasted Elk Lollipops

Bell's
Sparkling Ale

Sweet Potato Hash with Braised Pork Belly

Station 4
WOOD AGED & FRUIT

This "catch-all" category includes beers that have been wood-aged, brewed or conditioned with fruit and/or other ingredients with significant flavor impact. New and interesting flavor bridges occur with this innovative, "freestyle" collection of beers.

Short's
The Soft Parade

Pork Loin Stuffed with 'Funky Fruity' Chutney

Schmohz
Zingiberene Ale

Ahi Tuna with Asian Sesame Slaw

Jolly Pumpkin
Lambicus Dexterius

Duck Confit with Plum Sauce

Arcadia Brewing
Shipwreck Porter

New Holland
Dragon's Milk

Malted Milk Balls and Dragon's Milk Gelato

Thank you to the Executive Chef,
Wayne Wells and the Radisson's culinary team.

GRAZING

A collection of artisan cheeses, charcuterie, vegetables, spreads and salads
with an assortment of Michigan Beer.

LIBERTY STREET BREWING
IPA

CRANKER'S BREWERY
BULLDOG RED AMBER

PERRIN BREWING
GOLDEN ALE

RIGHT BRAIN BREWERY
BARREL AGED LOOPING OWL AMBER

PAW PAW BREWING
BLACK RIVER OATMEAL STOUT

DARK HORSE BREWING
SCOTTY KARATE SCOTCH ALE

NORTH PEAK BREWING
HOODOO MIDWESTERN WET HOP IPA

KEWEENAW BREWING
WIDOW MAKER BLACK LAGER

ATWATER BREWING
DETROIT PALE ALE

SAUGATUCK BREWING
SINGAPORE IPA

BELL'S BREWERY
LAGER OF THE LAKES

FOUNDERS BREWING
CENTENNIAL IPA

NEW HOLLAND BREWING
CABIN FEVER BROWN ALE

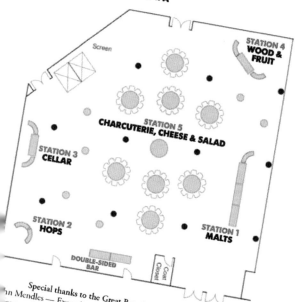

Special thanks to the Great Beer State Reception Team:
___n Mendles — Executive Chef, Jessie Wiebeck — Director of Banquets,
___eau — Banquet Bar Manager, Lindsay Davies — Special Events Producer, and
Fred Bueltmann, Beervangelist of New Holland Brewing.

THE GREAT BEER STATE RECEPTION & DINNER

WELCOME TO AN EVENING OF BEER & FOOD PAIRINGS

THURSDAY, JANUARY 10
7:00 P.M.

MIBEER.COM

MICHIGAN BREWERS GUILD AND MBAA - DISTRICT MICHIGAN WINTER CONFERENCE

JANUARY 9 - 11, 2013
RADISSON PLAZA HOTEL
KALAMAZOO, MI

MALT-FORWARD

The beers at this station feature the many flavors of brewers' malt. From grain-powered spiciness, caramel sweetness to coffee-laden roastiness, these beers are paired with foods that capitalize on these rich flavor-bridges.

FRANKENMUTH BREWING
WINTER BOCK
Braised Beef
on Spent Grain Bread
CHEBOYGAN BREWING
LIGHTHOUSE AMBER

WOLVERINE STATE BREWING
LAGER
Duck Eggs with Prosciutto,
Mustard Greens and Beer Bread
ROUND BARN BREWERY
KÖLSCH

FOUNDERS BREWING
PORTER
Beef Rib with Mushroom Ragu
and Beer Sauce
KEWEENAW BREWING
OLD OFF DOCK SCOTTISH ALE

SCHMOHZ BREWING
BONECRUSHER STOUT
Flourless Black Bean
Chocolate Cake
ARCADIA ALES
CEREAL KILLER BARLEYWINE

HOP-CENTRIC

This station features beer with hops as a significant part of their signature. The foods selected play off the aromatic, floral character, notes of grapefruit and playful bitterness.

BELL'S BREWERY
MIDWESTERN PALE ALE
"Adult Swim"
Smoked Mac & Cheese
DRAGONMEAD MICROBREWERY
CROWN JEWELS IPA

MT. PLEASANT BREWING
IPA
Curry Chicken Lollipops
with Asian Slaw
ARCADIA BREWING
HOPMOUTH DOUBLE IPA

DETROIT BEER COMPANY
BOHEMIAN PILSNER
Seared Tuna with Sriracha
and Pickled Daikon
NORTH PEAK BREWING
THE WANDERER IPA

BREWERY VIVANT
TRIOMPHE BELGIAN IPA
Citrus-Olive Oil Cake
with Candied Zest
SHORT'S BREWING
PONTIUS ROAD PILSNER

FROM THE CELLAR

These beers feature the flavors of fermentation. Yeast character, esters or other tastes of the cellar are prominent in the flavor profiles and the elements of the pairing.

TRI-CITY BREWING
FORTUNATO TRAPPIST ALE
Lamb Muhumbra
BELL'S BREWERY
OARSMAN

JOLLY PUMPKIN
CALABAZA BLANCA
Seared Scallops with
Caramelized Pearl Onions
and beer-braised greens
ARBOR BREWING
BOLLYWOOD BLONDE

ARBOR BREWING
FRAMBOOZLED SOUR BROWN ALE
Pork Belly Slider with
Arugula and Giardiniera
BREWERY VIVANT
SOLITUDE FARMHOUSE

DRAGONMEAD MICROBREWERY
FINAL ABSOLUTION TRIPEL
Brewer's Panettone with
Poached Pears and Figs
UNITY VIBRATIONS
GINGER KOMBUCHA

WOOD-AGED & FRUIT

This category includes beers that have been wood-aged, brewed or conditioned with fruit and/or other ingredients with significant flavor impact. New and interesting flavor bridges occur with this innovative, "freestyle" collection of beers.

FOUNDERS BREWING
BREAKFAST STOUT
Farrotto with
Roasted Mushrooms,
Grana Padano and Shallots
DARK HORSE BREWING
FORE SMOKED STOUT

NEW HOLLAND BREWING
DRAGON'S MILK
Smoked Duck Medallions
in Molé
JOLLY PUMPKIN
LA ROJA

NEW HOLLAND BREWING
CHARKOOTA RYE
Spice Roasted Turkey on
Cranberry Walnut Bread
SHORT'S BREWING
SOFT PARADE

ATWATER BREWERY
VANILLA JAVA PORTER
Beer-a-misu Parfait
SAUGATUCK BREWING
NEAPOLITAN STOUT

Braised Short Ribs Over Spätzle

Slow-cooked beef, like pot roasts and short ribs, is the original antidepressant. The aroma alone can lift you from the most serious case of Seasonal Affective Disorder. For those of you in warmer climates, you'll like it to, but for everyone else, it fills a bonafide need.

There's plenty of room to improvise here, so use what you have or what you like. I like splitting up the cooking liquid with both beer and stock. It gives you the best of both worlds and doesn't get too "beery." If you cook beer alone for this long, you risk unpleasant bitterness, as it will become unbalanced over time.

Serves 4-6

Short Ribs

2 tablespoon olive oil

4-5 lb. beef short ribs

1 tablespoon each salt and pepper

2 medium onions, peeled and chopped

3-4 carrots peeled and chopped

5 celery stalks, rinsed and chopped

1 head garlic, peeled

1 quart home-canned tomatoes, drained

24 oz. porter

4 cups stock (beef, chicken, or veggie)

3-4 sprigs thyme

2 bay leaves

Gravy

4 tablespoon butter

1/4 cup flour

Preheat oven to 300 degrees F. Combine salt and pepper and season short ribs liberally. Let sit and come to room temperature. Heat oil in cast iron Dutch oven on high heat, and add short ribs to brown on both sides. Remove from pan and set aside.

Combine mirepoix (onions, carrots, celery) in hot skillet, reducing heat to medium and tossing with salt to sweat 5-10 minutes until tender. Add tomatoes and garlic cloves and simmer for 5 minutes. Add beer and simmer for 25 minutes, reducing by about 1/3. Add thyme, bay leaf, and stock and bring to a boil.

Remove from heat and add ribs to Dutch oven. Cover with lid and cook in oven for 2 hours. Turn short ribs and cook uncovered for 45 minutes or longer, until fork tender.

Remove from oven. Remove ribs and place on sheet pan, straining and keeping the braising liquid in a separate bowl, pressing veggies to extract as much liquid as possible. Skim fat or pour into degreaser. Increase oven temperature to 450 degrees F.

Place sheet pan with ribs on top shelf of oven and roast for 10 minutes per side, browning and crisping the edges.

While the ribs are roasting, strain the braising liquid into a degreaser, or skim the fat for the jus. Taste for seasoning and hold warm.

Slice between finished ribs, and don't worry if the bones slip out—just leave them behind if they do. (It's a good thing.) Serve ribs over spätzle, generously topping with jus, serve with a tasty porter or oatmeal stout.

Braised Short Ribs Over Spätzle (cont.)

Traditional Spätzle:

2 1/4 cups all-purpose flour

1 teaspoon salt

1/4 teaspoon ground white pepper

1/8 teaspoon ground nutmeg

3 large eggs

3/4 cup whole milk

3 tablespoon fresh thyme, chopped

4 tablespoon butter, divided

2 tablespoon extra-virgin olive oil, divided

8 oz. mushrooms, thinly sliced

1 medium onion, chopped

3/4 cup beef or chicken stock

Blend flour, salt, pepper, and nutmeg in large bowl. Whisk in eggs and milk, forming soft batter. Mix in half the thyme.

Bring large pot of salted water to boil. Butter a large bowl and set aside. Press batter directly into boiling water through 1/4-inch holes on grater or other tool. Stir spaetzle to separate and boil 2 minutes. Scoop from pot, drain well, and transfer to buttered bowl and hold. (up to 3 hours)

Coffee Rubbed T-Bone

Dark beers and beef get along famously. I've always enjoyed using coffee to accentuate the roasty flavor bridges. These steaks should be able to handle plenty of beer intensity, so bring on the big stouts and let 'em come up a little in temperature. This is good on the grill or on a hot cast iron skillet, so choose based on preference or how high the snow is piled up. If you like it, the rub is handy on plenty of other cuts.

Serves 2-4

2–4 T-Bone Steaks or other bone-in cuts like ribeye and porterhouse.

1/3 cup dark coffee grounds

2 tablespoon kosher salt

2 tablespoon turbinado sugar

1/3 cup smoked paprika

Preheat grill. Combine coffee, paprika, and salt and sugar. Generously rub steaks and allow to sit at room temperature for 15 minutes or more. Grill on medium-high heat, turning every 4-5 minutes until desired temperature is reached. Serve with barrel-aged dark beer.

Drinking Winter

Malt: Porters and Stouts

Stouts feature flavors born from dark, malted, and/or roasted barley. When barley is malted, it is steeped, germinated, and kilned. Brewers have access to various malts that have been kilned to different degrees. As with coffee, to get the darkest color and deepest flavor, barley and other grains are roasted at higher heats. The flavors developed include elements of coffee, chocolate, and charred notes. By increasing the amount and/or number of dark malts in their recipe, brewers create dark beers rich in character and flavor.

I find stouts are often overlooked by casual beer drinkers, who may assume, based on the color, that they should expect a heavy, cumbersome sip. I encourage all to explore the subtlety and nuance behind the dark veil of intrigue that is a delicious glass of stout. They are often lighter on their feet than they appear and showcase depth of flavor that is inviting to all, including supposed non-beer drinkers.

Dark malts provide delicious counterpoint between rich sweetness and roasty bitterness. Sweetness in stouts and porters is often expressed as chocolate, while bitterness can taste coffee-like with its deep, roasted character. Of course, stouts are the mutts of the beer world, with hybrids, variations, and interpretations spanning centuries.

The line between porters and stouts has been blurred by history, variation, and brewer interpretation.

The Wide World of Stouts:

- Stout—Classic malted barley, coffee, and chocolate tones, medium body.
- Porter—More cocoa and caramel present, less roasty than stout.
- Dry (Irish) Stout— Often "nitrogenated," or carbonated and dispensed with the aid of nitrogen. Creamy, cocoa, and roasted barley flavors, with light to medium body.
- Oatmeal Stout—Oats lend creaminess and softness to classic roasty stout flavors.
- Sweet (Milk) Stout—Typically, unfermentable milk sugar (lactose) is used to lend a harmonious sweetness to the dark malt flavor.
- Imperial Stout—The use of "Imperial" as a style designation began here, as stouts were brewed extra strong to avoid freezing en route from England to Russia. Strong, bold flavors and big body with edgy roastiness.

Stouts and porters can contrast with dairy or act as a cleansing contrast to spicy heat, like cayenne. They're also great with dairy in the same way chocolate complements vanilla ice cream, or coffee goes with cream. Mushrooms and beef will conjure their savory earthiness. There is a wide range in intensity amongst styles and brands, so use your big, bad Imperials with robust foods, and head towards the more medium-bodied for more easygoing pairs.

Hops: Imperial IPAs

Imperial or Double IPAs borrow their title from the historic Russian Imperial Stout. The Imperial designation is used interchangeably with "Double," and it indicates a robust interpretation of the IPA style with intense character and plenty of alcohol. These beers are typically over 10% in alcohol and come packing some heat. They showcase hops in all of their glory, bringing punctuated bitterness, hop flavor, and aroma. These hop flavors can range from earthy and herbal to big citrus, especially grapefruit.

In order to balance this intense hop bitterness, these beers are typically very big in body and malt character as well, although their maltiness is perceived in a supporting role, and thus is not prominent on our palate's first impression. Bridging to the malt will bring the sweetness forward, and thus usually relax the beer a bit. More than any other style, I feel like these beers are in their best light when served with food.

Cellar: Sour Ales

I like to think of sour ales as outlaw beers, as they dare to break rules in compelling, flavorful ways with intriguing depth of character.

There are several styles of sours, and within those, tons of individual interpretations and variations. They present varying degrees of tartness, fruit-like esters, and tannic character, or even vinegar (acetic) qualities. Depending on the style, they may be subtle or assertive, from golden or red to brown and black.

I often describe the allure of sour ales using the "blue cheese theory." Cheese you left in the fridge too long, that got a little furry? Not an outlaw, and not blue cheese. A hunk of cheese intentionally inoculated with veins of blue mold running through it? Stinky and delicious! What blue cheese, sour ales, and vinegar have in common is that, artfully controlled, enough of an otherwise bad thing (bacteria) becomes good again. Hauntingly good.

Largely Belgian-inspired, sour ales are the result of wild yeasts and/or bacteria being introduced to the beer. These little buggers are similar to normal brewing yeasts, but they have a wider diet, eating a larger range of sugars and carbs, creating many intense flavor compounds and sourness as a result. These beers are often warm-conditioned in wood barrels to encourage these voracious yeasts and bacteria to go to work, allowing the beer's character to go from curious to sublime.

Here's a list of a few styles with some typical characteristics, but any sour ale should be poured with an open mind. Look for the dance between sweet brewing malts, bright tartness, and often woody, mineral-esque notes in-between.

Lambics & Geuze. These styles originated in Belgium and are fermented with wild yeasts and bacteria from the air, introduced by exposing the cooling, unfermented wort using a "coolship." The intensity varies greatly, and Geuze blends young and old lambics, often with the addition of fruit. Be on the lookout for fruit labeled in their native French, such as kriek (cherry) and framboise (raspberry).

Flanders Red (AKA Flemish). These beers are assertively tart, a vivid contrast to their rich malt character. They may range from red to brown and are typically effervescent and brightly acetic.

Berlinner Weisse. A light wheat ale with lower alcohol and golden color. Bright tartness frames an otherwise soft session beer. A lively carbonation is frequently augmented at the bar with flavored syrups such as raspberry or woodruff.

Wood and Fruit: Barrel-Aged

"Barrel-aged" is a phrase you see more and more these days, as many brewers borrow and coerce flavors from various types of barrels. Any style of beer can go into one of several different types of barrels. Fresh barrels are usually oak, and their insides have been toasted or charred to various degrees, which can be selected by the purchasing brewery, winery, or distillery. More often than not, a barrel-aged beer is introduced into a barrel that has already held another liquid, often bourbon, wine, rum, sherry, or brandy. After the beer goes in, it actually penetrates the wood, replacing some of the spirit and leeching spirit back to the center. Brewers manage time, temperature, and humidity to arrive at the desired exchange of flavors.

The beers take on really interesting characters, depending on all of these decisions. Compounds within the wood include vanilla and coconut-like flavors. Lying beneath the primary compounds, there are also tannins that can give interesting structure and depth to the beers. Brewers can combine many barrels into a batch, or simply select a single barrel, depending on what they're looking for in intensity and volume.

As I mentioned in "Sour Ales," wood aging can also be used to sour beers intentionally. The mischievous yeast and bacteria are kept in check with handling and refrigeration for this collection of beers, so we're talking about the flavor impact of charred wood and residual spirit more than anything else.

The styles vary quite a bit, as it's a fun place for brewers to experiment. Stouts seem to be the most common and, as you likely already know, I have a great affinity for them. My brewery's beer, Dragon's Milk, is a bourbon barrel stout, and it is particularly close to my heart. Barrel-aged stouts most frequently use bourbon barrels, as the sweetness combines beautifully with the oaky tannins and vanilla. I find that barrel aging provides smooth, round edges, making a complex beer feel cozy and poetic. These beers pair with extreme agility. The tannic structure gives them a bridge to balsamic vinegar or the foods you enjoy with balsamic. As a stout, they're already great with mushrooms and beef and, with oaky vanilla in the game, they feel velvety smooth and decadent. I also feel barrel-aged stout is a textbook example of umami, as the earthiness of mushroom and woodsy notes from the barrel combine for a beer experience that is transcendent and indescribable. There is a kinship between the lurking, subconscious charred notes from barrel aging and smoked foods. It seems counterintuitive at first, but connecting food and drink that were born of burned wood will make you happy.

These barrel-aged dark beers are also a wonderful invitation to red wine drinkers. Many people attempt to find a beer for wine drinkers, especially female wine drinkers, by going to lighter beers. Surely they need a beginner beer to bring them in slowly. If they didn't grow up drinking beer, or never liked it, their palate senses these beers and their bright bitterness as foreigners, and sends them packing. If we find out beginners like red wine, coffee, and chocolate, and we think about their palate memory, we realize these dark, woodsy beers are a wonderful fit. The tannic structure and oaky notes, blended with malty tones of chocolate and coffee, have redefined what beer is for some people who "didn't know beer could do that!"

If that isn't enough, dessert is this beer's wheelhouse. It is a go-to beer, even if you don't think too hard about composing around flavor bridges. It will reward thoughtful composition, of course, with layers upon layers of flavor, often developing with each sip and each bite.

Ambers or brown ales are likely the next most popular barrel-aged beers that you'll find at retail. They also connect these wonderful flavors together, usually with a slighter influence from the barrel, so as to leave the malt components intact and up front.

Lamb Liver Mousse

I enjoy the irony that rustic, farmhouse foods have become our current delicacies. Charcuterie is essentially the art of putting meat up by cooking and using preservation techniques. It was the farmers and butchers who found ways to use every bit of the animal. They either created these dishes or preserved them by carrying on the traditional methods.

I love it all, cooked, cured, or smoked: sausages, rillettes, prosciutto, and speck. I am not well-versed in making it all, but every year I get a little more ambitious. This mousse was inspired by a traditional chicken liver mousse, which you might also call pâté. I adapted it as a pair for our Blue Sunday Sour. I love the contrast of the smooth, rich indulgence of the mousse against the bracing tartness and complex malt of a sour ale. I consider the sour ale as taking on the role that pickled onions or chutneys often play on a charcuterie plate.

Serves 6-8

2 cups lamb livers

2 tablespoon minced shallots

2 tablespoon butter

1/3 cup bourbon

1/4 cup bourbon barrel stout

1/4 cup whipping cream

1/2 teaspoon salt

1/2 teaspoon allspice

1/2 teaspoon pepper

Pinch thyme

1/2 cup melted butter

2 tablespoon pork fat, melted

Trim the livers, removing dark spots, and slice into 1/2-inch pieces. Sauté in butter with shallots until stiffened, but still rosy. Remove to blender and hold.

Combine bourbon and stout in sauté pan and reduce to 3 tablespoons of sticky goodness. Add to liver and shallots in blender.

Add heavy cream, salt, allspice, pepper, and thyme to the livers and blend on high speed to a smooth paste. Add the melted butter and pork fat and blend again.

Pour/press though strainer into a separate bowl and taste for seasoning.

Line the bottom of a terrine pan with parchment paper and butter the sides. Fill terrine with mousse, cover and chill for several hours. Unmold to serve.

Lamb Stew

I buy fresh, local lamb every year, and it usually arrives in early Winter. The stew meat cooks wonderfully, and I enjoy the sweet earthiness it gives to all the good veggies in it. Herbs are an important part of this stew and really round out the beautiful lamb character, making this a great dish for many palates. I love it with porters, but you can easily head to browns and ambers as well.

This stew is a similar build or technique to the other stews in the book, but with a slightly different flavor profile. I encourage improvisation and variation, so feel free to adjust quantities, adding or replacing ingredients as you choose. The beer adds a nice layer of depth, but is also optional.

Serves 6-8

1 lb. lamb stew meat, seasoned with salt and pepper

2 medium onions, chopped

2 carrots, sliced

2-3 parsnips, cut into cubes

1-2 potatoes, cut into cubes

1 quart of canned tomatoes, drained and chopped

1 teaspoon cumin

1 teaspoon thyme, dried (increase to 1 tablespoon if fresh)

1 teaspoon marjoram, dried (increase to 1 tablespoon if fresh)

Pinch of salt and pepper

3 cups beef stock

1 cup porter or stout

Sweat salted onions and carrots in oil on medium-high heat in a cast iron Dutch oven or saucepan. In 5-10 minutes, when vegetables are tender, brown the stew meat before adding parsnips, potatoes, tomatoes, spices, salt, and pepper. When bubbling and hot, add stock and beer. Bring to a high simmer, just before the boil; cover and reduce to low heat and cook for 1 1/2-2 hours. Taste and adjust seasoning. Serve over barley (see roasted pork recipe on page 67) or brown rice with porters, smooth stouts, or brown ale.

The Dichotomy of Craft

Here is another rant that pits the two sides of my brain against each other. A large part of the craft renaissance is a result of small, independent brewers, distillers, and food producers fighting tooth and nail against the norms that were installed in our culture over a period of industrialization and nationalization of our food and drink. The big companies that grew out of this period created the market conditions that lowered prices, and thus the value of food and drink, and created commoditization by narrowing the range of flavor and diversity. This was not on accident or because they lacked any technical efficiency; this was a long-term strategy that serves them well as long as they dominate or even monopolize the market.

These conditions have been and remain a threat to quality and are very damaging to the creative independent who wants to make something beautiful, charge a fair price for it, and find a space to sell it in the marketplace. It is important not only to give credit to the revolutionary craft producers who have brought craft back into play, but also to remember that it was, and still is, a fight for quality. We are making huge progress, but craft beer is still a serious minority, accounting for less than 7% of the beer sold in the U.S. Progress or not, we must remember who created these conditions and know that, unchecked, they will undoubtedly worsen, creating fewer players, less concern for creative, artistic processes, and less choice overall. It's quite a soapbox, I know, and if we have a chance to have this conversation over a beer, it'll climb atop it with even more gusto.

The dichotomy is that this idea, however valid and crucial, is a contrast to my flavor-first philosophy. While we develop and please our palates, there are times to separate the brand champion and political activist side of our brain and just taste. It's the whole "your brain is a liar" piece when it comes to tasting. If we go into a beverage expecting to hate it because we revile the company's ethics or business practices, we can certainly convince our palate it tastes terrible.

If we communicate this bias, or a sense of inferior product, to others, whether talking with friends or leading a guided tasting, it may well be that it won't match what's in the glass. Another beer drinker, who may not share the same level of awareness about the company, is not necessarily going to taste our contempt, and the description may fall flat or seem inaccurate.

As an ambassador for craft beer, I've never felt that judgment is an inviting posture. I refuse to bash someone for whatever they've been drinking for the last however many years. I don't feel we welcome people to the flavor and quality of craft by telling them they've been doing it wrong and making bad decisions. I'd rather ask good questions and learn what part of the experience from those beers was important to them, and guide them towards a flavor journey from there. The duality of these ideas can be confusing, especially for an old timer like myself.

If you want to choose where to spend your dollars based on ethics and company ideals, that is admirable, but a wholly different conversation than a palate-based decision on flavor alone. I do think we should make our purchasing decisions based on a connection to and trust of the producer. There are many reasons to care about who makes your food and drink, and large, international conglomerates have proven they have difficulties maintaining a concern for the consumer as part of their culture. We have good reason to trust that they won't care for our quality of life or quality of choice. With current trends in the marketplace valuing quality, sourcing, and artisan production, we see many of these companies masquerading as craft, in both food and drink. If you are passionate about this part of our industry and culture, it is important to read labels, follow the industry, and champion ethics by voting with your dollars.

I believe in attempting to separate those political views from my flavor experience. This doesn't mean I necessarily want to drink the beers or support companies owned by the giant companies that have intentionally tried to thwart the craft movement for as long as I can remember. It means that I will not confuse my palate by allowing these opinions to influence my flavor experience and create palate bias. Tasting blind is a great way to work these muscles and remind yourself to taste objectively. This may also help us as professionals to understand the beers our potential customers are drinking and to be better equipped to create bridges for them to appropriate craft beers that will be a good fit for their palates.

The Holidays

The holidays are times of great socialization. We visit with friends and family, we laugh, we cry and, in many cases, we enjoy a drink or two together. There is no possible way to capture what is appropriate for all holidays or all families, but I thought I'd set out a few suggestions that might make your celebration that much more flavorful and enjoyable.

Variety is the spice of life. One of the things I love about holiday parties and dinners is there is often a wide range of food and drink. If you're hosting or bringing beer to the party, consider bringing several styles of beer. This might include your go-to styles, but it's also a time to explore several of the specialties available, including spiced Christmas ales and other unique concoctions.

Beer is for sharing, and these rolling events with a variety of people are prime times to share. Be sure to provide glasses near the beer station, not only because they're more enjoyable to drink from, but because they allow and encourage sampling. People can try just a sip of something, or make their rounds through the available selections by pouring smaller servings, without having to drink a full beer of each. It's not a bad idea to provide smaller glassware, especially if the beers are stronger than normal, so people don't accidentally over-serve themselves.

Whether you're at a dinner table or mingling at an open house, it's a great time for large bottles. They work the sharing and variety angle, and obviously pour more glasses per bottle, thus creating less waste and clutter on a bar or beverage table. You may need to seed the idea by opening a couple of bottles and leaving them near the glasses, as not everyone is accustomed to the practice.

These get-togethers are perfect for digging into your cellar and pulling out rare, special, or even forgotten beers, large or small. If you want to share the experience with people, you may want to keep them tucked away until the right moment for you to pour for people. It's a gift that is as much fun to give as to receive, and an opportunity for more people to be able to taste something special, even if it's only from one bottle.

It is always good form to pour special beers with no strings attached, meaning you have to be OK if people don't like it or maybe don't even note the degree of specialness. During the holidays it's even more important to keep a relaxed attitude because there will usually be a wide variety of people with varied beer experience. A lot of these special beers, barleywines, barrel-aged treats of all kinds, and spiced ales might appeal to drinkers used to wine or spirits, and a small casual pour gives them room to try beer instead. If we overdo the explanations or reverence, we risk appearing elitist, snobby, or just plain off-putting, and that is not part of the holiday spirit.

Beer makes a great gift, too. It's a great excuse to splurge on an indulgent case or two of something outside of your normal routine and split it up, giving single bottles, four packs, or whatever to your surprised and grateful friends and family. You can also save a little something special for entertaining or for your cellar.

Beervangelist's Guide to the Galaxy

If you're bringing a beer gift to a party, let them know if you'd like them to save it or drink it tonight. If you want them to save it, suggest that they put it away so they can have it another time, or think about hanging an obvious tag on it. If you'd like to share it with them, look for a good moment to round up some glasses and encourage a pour. Otherwise, sit back and let it all flow. It's the holidays—there's bound to be another tasty glass of beer headed your way soon.

Beer vs. Wine

On the beer versus wine front, I consider myself equal parts pacifist and beer militant. I have nothing against wine; in fact, I enjoy it a great deal and respect the artistry of winemaking. I especially love its connection all the way back to the soil and season. That's the pacifist talking.

Throngs of people have been part of the huge craft beer renaissance that has been going on for more than a decade and has intensified a great deal in the most recent years. Even so, beer still fights at a deficit for our greater culture's attention and respect, which activates my beer militant persona. As a professional beer guy for a very long time, I am far too aware of our tendency to relegate beer to the bar or ball game and shift directly to wine as the established drink for dinner. "Red or white?" has been an iconic question at the dinner table for a long time, and I've marveled at the clever way it asks a question while quietly inserting the assumption, "You're drinking wine, we just have yet to establish the color."

You would be surprised at the number of times I've seen the look of wonder and surprise as people hear about beer at a tasting party with cheese or chocolate. "You mean, like a wine pairing?" I suppose my ego is involved, as I want to stand up for beer's honor and say, "Yes, only better." The point is that yes, beer is every bit as capable of any level of sophistication, and I object to the surprise that reveals the limiting opinion of beer. I generally set my objection aside and gently and non-sarcastically confirm that yes, despite the nonexistent, yet apparently complicated challenges, beer can be drunk next to various foods.

Believe it or not, the cultural smirk or condescending head pat is still alive and well in the restaurant world as well. It lives in that moment

when you mention you'd like beer with dinner and the server looks at you like you're the Jed Clampett of fine dining. Granted, we have many more people upping their game than ever before, and I am optimistic and grateful. I don't want to stop, however, with the relatively small portion of people who believe beer deserves its place at the table. I want to continue to Beervangelize with my colleagues until every restaurant in every town gives beer equal or greater consideration than given to wine or spirits when working on menus and training.

I feel I've made a strong case for beer's ability to enhance a meal. Choosing a beverage is a simple, instinctive process, yet yields so much complexity and depth if we consider broader choices than "red or white?" Honestly, the question or the answer doesn't always have to be beer, either. The best hosts and best servers in this world will be prepared to offer quality options for wine, spirits, and beer. Beauty, grace, and wonderful flavor bridges are in all types of beverages, and we should keep an open mind. Flavor is without limits, so enjoy for yourself and as you please.

Pink Christmas

I volunteered to help my parents with a Christmas potluck they were hosting for the first time. It was a gathering for many extended family members on Christmas Day that had always been at my Grandfather's, prior to his passing. Twenty or thirty people would attend, socializing and catching up, with a buffet meal served in the late afternoon.

I offered to cook the turkey and help coordinate the kitchen so my Mom didn't have to worry about it and the turkey didn't have to travel. It was an oddly simple task, as this was the potluck of all potlucks.

I prepared the turkey as usual, in a beer brine with the fennel rub. I started it early, in my parents' oven, which had a convection option. I had used commercial convection ovens in the past; and they seriously reduce cooking time, as they aggressively blow heat around the chamber of the oven. I credit my brine for saving Thanksgiving a couple years prior, as the commercial convection oven I was using cooked the turkey so fast, I was twenty degrees past my target the first time I checked it. Without the brine, that turkey would have been dry as toast, but instead, it was still moist and tender.

This one looked and smelled beautiful, as I took a temperature read, that showed it well ahead of schedule. I figured the convection oven had been working its magic again. I set the turkey to rest and got ready for the guests and other dishes to arrive.

The house filled up as everyone exchanged their Christmas greetings. I helped warm things and get all the dishes on the serving table while we waited for my Uncle to arrive, as the family tradition calls for him to carve the turkey. Shortly after he started carving, he called me over. "Uh, Fred, I think we have a problem here." I looked to see that as he cut alongside the leg, the turkey was pink. "Maybe, it's just be the color of the brine... that can be misleading," I thought out loud. Nope, it wasn't the brine. The turkey was severely undercooked, and every other dish was on the table, with a crowd of hungry guests and a kitchen full of holiday traffic.

It's a cook's nightmare. I started to grasp the major error in judgment I had made, and I could feel the blood running to my flushed face, as I tried to process the problem amidst the sea of guests. Through my red-faced embarrassment and slight panic, I hatched a plan. I worked with my Uncle and we quickly broke the turkey down, cutting it into parts, returning wrapped pieces to the oven. I was counting on the smaller pieces cooking faster, and the foil wrap preventing them from drying out. In a little more than a half hour, we were serving cooked, carved turkey, and the party moved on.

As everyone ate, the kitchen discussion inevitably revolved around the mishap. I received pointers and suggestions and questions about why or how it happened. I tried to receive it all graciously but I also wanted to jump out of the window from the embarrassment of it all. I kept asking myself, "how did this happen?"

It all boiled down to taking a bad read on the thermometer. I thought it was odd and was surprised the turkey was so far ahead of schedule, but figured the convection oven could be responsible, so I moved on and embraced the idea of a longer rest. Maybe "potluck mode" put me off my game, but whatever the case, I made a bad call.

I should have trusted my instincts above the tool. Had I looked for more information by touching the bird, checking the leg with a few more wiggles, or taking a few more reads with the thermometer, I would have corrected myself, and avoided this problem altogether. I also could have trusted the brine and been more comfortable in cooking slightly past my target, knowing the bird would still be moist.

I'm reminded of our second Porkapalooza, a pig, beer, and music fest we hosted on the farm a few years ago. Neighbor Matt and I were committed to cooking a pig luau-style, burying it in the earth on coals for the day. As the time to serve it approached, and with hundreds of people looking forward to it, Matt showed me the remote thermometer, which read just over 100 degrees. I bravely quipped, "That's not pork, that's a pig with a fever!" To this day, I am grateful that Matt laughed rather than burying me with the pig after that remark. He and his team responded to the problem by quickly putting a plan B into action, digging up the pig, butchering it, and grilling it in parts. It was a plan that was disappointing to them, but it also ripped success from the snarling teeth of failure.

Both of these stories involve the challenge of moving through emotions of frustration, fear and insecurity when we feel we're at risk, or worse yet, when shit heads South. Across all levels of experience, all cooks have their disaster stories.

Moments like these call on us to set aside our pride and remember that we're cooking for someone beside ourselves. A good cook will figure out how to get something tasty to the table, no matter what. A good host will find their sense of humor, throwing away disclaimers and insecurities so they can entertain gracefully, even in the face of a cooking disaster.

Beer & Dessert

Beer at the dinner table as a versatile, meal-enhancing beverage is not a new idea. Beer is catching the attention of chefs, sommeliers, cicerones, and the food and drink media. Its popularity notwithstanding, it's still common to get a raised eyebrow from a diner when one suggests beer for the meal's finale, dessert. Familiar desserts and the flavor bridges found in craft beer demonstrate that beer is actually the most versatile, elegant, and ultimately best-suited companion you could possibly dream up for dessert. Let's review some flavor families and think about how they help bring beer to the dessert table.

Malt-forward beers typically feature one or more of the following: roast, caramel, chocolate, coffee, toffee, molasses, toastiness, and nuttiness. Almost sounds like we're writing a dessert recipe, doesn't it?

Stouts feature dark, roasty tones that complement chocolate and coffee desserts or contrast with creamy custards, gelatos, and ice cream. They offer deep contrast to fruits and berries known for their delicious counterpart to chocolate: strawberries, raspberries, and cherries.

Barleywines and wheatwines present caramel, nut and/or molasses flavors. Complement caramelized sugars in dessert (crème brûlée, crisps, pie crusts), or contrast with chocolate and vanilla. These robust beers appear delicate and light-footed with the right dessert.

Hop-centric beers feature floral aromatics, citrus (grapefruit & lime), and acidity. Although rare at dessert, hops can be a delightful surprise. Go for big beers, Double/Imperial IPAs that bring malt sweetness and strong citrus along with the hops. Bridge to profiles like key-lime, mint, or grapefruit. A secret weapon with blue cheese.

From the Cellar. Fermentation-forward beers showcase the fruity esters (banana, apple, apricot) and spiciness created from their specific yeasts' flavor production during fermentation. These beers can be sweet, tart, sour, or dry.

Tripels and hefe weizens bring in banana or clove, a great accent for berries and medium-bodied desserts like tarts or tuiles.

Saisons, wheats, and white ales pair subtly. Look for citrus bridges and light or savory-influenced desserts.

Wood-aged and fruit-conditioned beers bring in additional ingredients, techniques, and flavors. Wood can bring vanilla, spirit, and oakiness. Fruit can flavor, sweeten, sour, or brighten a beer.

Beervangelist's Guide to the Galaxy

Lambics with fruit or other fruit beers are excellent dessert beers. Don't feel you have to pair fruit with fruit. Substitute/deconstruct using the fruit's known counterparts. For example, a raspberry beer would go well with a dish compatible with raspberry sauce, like chocolate mousse.

Oak-aged beers add vanilla and wood to their original profiles. These beers make hitting one or more of the Four Cs easy. Fruit, chocolate, cream, and vanilla are all worth a shot with a balanced wood-aged beer.

I find dessert to be both an elegant setting for beer and and a very grounding and personal course. It is a great time to share beers, no matter the bottle size, pouring small, three-to-four-ounce servings in your favorite stemware. Also, it's a great time to let the beer come to "cellar temperature," a little warmer than your refrigerator. Beer is often so harmonious with dessert that the flavor sensations can be ethereal, working into a whole body experience with goose bumps, neck shivers, and involuntary sighs and shakes of the head.

Bourbon Stout Cake

I've always enjoyed trying to recreate favorite restaurant dishes with nothing more than a fond memory. This cake is inspired by a five-year-old memory of a Stout Cake made by my good friends at the legendary Journeyman Cafe in my hometown.

I imagined the rich, dense chocolate that was both intense and agile, graceful yet powerful. This cake welcomes you to just dive into the chocolate and let go. Dark, roasty beers are welcome here. From medium-bodied porters to big, bad Imperial stouts, it's hard to go wrong.

Cakes:

2 cups The Poet Oatmeal Stout (or similar)

1/2 lb. unsalted butter

1 1/2 cups unsweetened cocoa powder

4 cups all-purpose flour

4 cups sugar

1 tablespoon baking soda

1 1/2 teaspoon kosher salt

4 large eggs, at room temperature

1 tablespoon pure vanilla extract

1 1/3 cups sour cream

Ganache Icing:

2 cups heavy whipping cream

1 pound semisweet chocolate, chopped

2 tablespoon Beer Barrel Bourbon

Dark brown sugar, as needed

Chocolate shavings (optional)

Directions:

Preheat the oven to 350 degrees F. Line the bottoms of three buttered 8-inch pans with parchment paper.

Bring the stout and butter to a simmer, whisking in the cocoa powder until smooth. Remove from heat and allow to cool.

In a separate bowl, whisk together the flour, sugar, baking soda, and salt.

In the bowl of an electric mixer, beat the eggs, vanilla, and sour cream on low. Add the stout and flour mixtures while beating on low into an even consistency. Pour the batter evenly into the prepared pans.

Bake the cakes in the preheated oven for 35-50 minutes. When done, set the cake pans on a wire rack to cool.

Ganache Icing:

In a double-boiler or a stainless bowl over steam, melt the chocolate in cream and bourbon. Whisk until smooth. Taste and sweeten as necessary with dark sugar. Cover and refrigerate until icing reaches spreadable consistency.

Putting it all together:

Build a 3-layer cake by spreading icing between layers. Once built, continue to cover sides and top of entire cake. Top with chocolate shavings or other garnish.

Dragon's Milk Doughnut

The Dragon's Milk Doughnut is personal. I designed it as part of a whole hog dinner at Black Dog Smokehouse in Champaign, IL, which had invited me to guest chef. I enjoyed the challenge and was pretty content to have creatively incorporated bacon into a dessert. I originally named it "Homer's Delight," as it seemed so over the top, and I could just hear Homer saying, "Mmmmmm, bacon doughnut..." After experiencing the doughnut, however, "Homer" didn't seem to do it justice, as it tasted casual, sophisticated, and luxurious, if I do say so myself.

The doughnut recipe itself went through many incarnations, as I just wasn't satisfied with how the various doughs were finishing in the fryer. I researched the vast world of the doughnut and donut debates, and each version was good—but it wasn't quite there yet. I was pretty set on adapting a beignet recipe, and the night before I was cooking them for an important event, I ran this idea past my good friend and local chef Matt Pietsch, while I dined at his restaurant. He grabbed a napkin and scribbled out a quick recipe, explaining that it was the beignet recipe that was passed down to him. As you might imagine, the impassioned cocktail napkin recipe kicked exhaustive research's ass, and the Dragon's Milk Doughnut was finally complete.

All of the other dishes in this book have beer recommendations that include broad style suggestions which could be met with several brands. For this one, I have only one suggestion: Dragon's Milk.

Dragon's Milk Doughnut (cont.)

Serves 6-8

Doughnut (Beignet)

16 oz. whole milk

8 oz. butter

Pinch salt

Pinch sugar

10 oz. bread flour

6 eggs

Combine milk, butter, salt, and sugar into a saucepan and bring just to a boil. Add flour, whisk, then stir until it comes away from the side of the pan. Transfer to bowl of an electric mixer with whip attachment.

Mix on medium, adding one egg at a time, increasing speed towards end.

Drop spoonfuls of batter into 350 degree F oil for 6-8 minutes until golden brown.

Dragon's Milk Sauce

1 cup Dragon's Milk

1/2 cup turbinado sugar

2 tablespoon butter

Reduce over medium-high heat, whisking until desired consistency. Set aside to cool; fill piping bag or syringe.

Custard

5 egg yolks

1 cup sugar

1/4 cup Dragon's Milk

1/2 cup flour

2 cups milk, brought to a boil

1 tablespoon butter

1/2 oz. bourbon

1 oz. Dragon's Milk

Beat yolks until thick; beat in sugar, followed by 1/4 cup Dragon's Milk until thickened to ribbon consistency. Beat in 1/2 cup flour. Beat in 2 cups boiling milk.

Whip over heat to boil; remove from heat, stirring in 1 tablespoon butter, 1/2 oz. whiskey, and 1 oz. Dragon's Milk (to taste and consistency). Fill piping bag or food syringe.

Bacon Praline

2 parts brown sugar

1 part almonds

8 strips of bacon

Pulse in food processor until uniformly chopped. Heat strips of bacon on foil-covered sheet pans in a 375 degree F oven for 7 minutes. Top with sugar/almond mixture. Continue to bake 5 minutes.

Drain and cool completely. Slice into chunks, add to food processor bowl. Process until uniformly crumbled. Add more sugar/pecan mix to taste or desired balance. Set aside to toss.

The Build:

Inject custard into cooled doughnuts using piping bag and top with Dragon's Milk sauce. Dust with bacon praline.

Happy Pigs

The shots were true. In a moment, the 275-pound, black-haired pigs we knew as Kevin and Frances Bacon were gone. It's difficult to summarize my experience with this, as it's really the culmination of many months. I am sure it changes with familiarity, but this first venture into hog butchery has been poignant, revealing, and quite inspirational.

One of the most surprising shifts in perspective was how our sense of responsibility fueled not only our decisions, but dramatically shaped our level of "being OK" with it all. At our farm, Red Horse Ranch, my wife Ulla and I have a fair amount of visitors and, for the last six months, most of them were introduced to the pigs.

After petting them, scratching their backs, and perhaps enjoying the marvel of the pigs basking in the cool spray of a garden hose or dropping themselves into a kiddie pool, the inevitable questions were something like, "These are pets, right?" or, "How are you going to eat them?" or, "Did you name them? I heard you're not supposed to name the animals you're gonna eat..."

What's important to note here is that none of these questions were out of line or in a negative light. The theme was curiosity and a bit of reservation, I believe, as people wondered whether they could do it. We had a few vegetarians who would change the conversation slightly, but we were never challenged as if there was anything wrong with what we were doing, and we appreciate all of our friends and visitors and their willingness to speak openly.

When visiting other farms, near cute animals that were being raised for meat, I've heard various farmers answer the question, "How can you get to know them when you know..." The farmers I admire have answered with essentially the same answer: "How could I not?"

While I appreciated and agreed with that answer, I don't think I fully understood it until now. Think about it: if we eat meat or use leather, we are involved in the cycle of life that involves capitalizing on an animal's loss of life. Sounds blunt, but those are the facts. As a civilized, human society, though, we seem to have put a lot of distance between us and that reality.

I'm not going to head into a meat-eating vs. vegetarian discussion; I want to simply point out that if we're meat eaters, we're already "in." Consciously or not, we've accepted this cycle. How it plays out is now up to whomever we've authorized to handle the animals that contribute to our lifestyle.

This is where everything flips on its head. As I grew closer to this idea and as we cared for these animals, "How could I not?" would bubble up in my head. As I got more acclimated to these pigs' place in the cycle—they were bred for this ultimate end—a sense of responsibility set the tone. Basically, quality of life became more important than length of life. These animals would spend their life on our farm before filling our freezer, and I had not only the responsibility, but also the opportunity, to give them a high-quality of life as part of the deal.

There's this contrary notion that one should divorce oneself from getting close to animals that will be harvested and, while it's completely understandable, it seems a bit unfair. If I'm going to claim my place on the food chain and take this animal's life, I feel compelled and obligated to enrich the moments it is alive with health and affection, rather than the other way around.

Our pigs feasted on beautiful produce scraps from our kitchen and from our local restaurant, which also tossed in leftover bread. They drank whey from our local creamery and enjoyed plenty of local fruit as well. They had fresh air, good dirt, and plenty of back scratches and belly rubs. As the date drew closer, I started serving them beer, first some leftover harvest ale and then their final week's indulgence, daily rations of The Poet Oatmeal Stout.

Our sense of responsibility carried through to the final day. We dropped them in the pen they were raised in, without an ounce of adrenaline or fear in their hearts. We utilized traditional methods, albeit with some challenges, to be able to use every part of the animal. As the five or six of us labored for hours in the bone-chilling, damp cold, working through some rookie frustrations, the feelings that resounded in me were gratefulness and obligation. I am grateful for the relationship between the animals and us. I am obligated to honor that with the process, my cooking, and the care of future animals.

It is completely reasonable to not want to be this involved emotionally or physically in the raising of your food. It is reasonable to choose not to get your hands dirty in order to eat well, or to support sustainable farming. I am changed for the better by this experience, and whether you ever raise or butcher meat yourself or not, please remember that someone does.

I am past the point of questioning whether we as humans can take another animal's life. What we need to question is how they are treated while they're being raised. We must honor and support the cycle of life with healthy, pleasant, and caring conditions that raise happy animals. Whether you're buying meat or raising it, we are all in the cycle and can make a difference with our voices and our decisions.

If we slow down to think about the context of how animals are raised when we make our buying decisions, we'll naturally make the right and reasonable call and choose to support farms that raise happy animals, as a matter of health and respect.

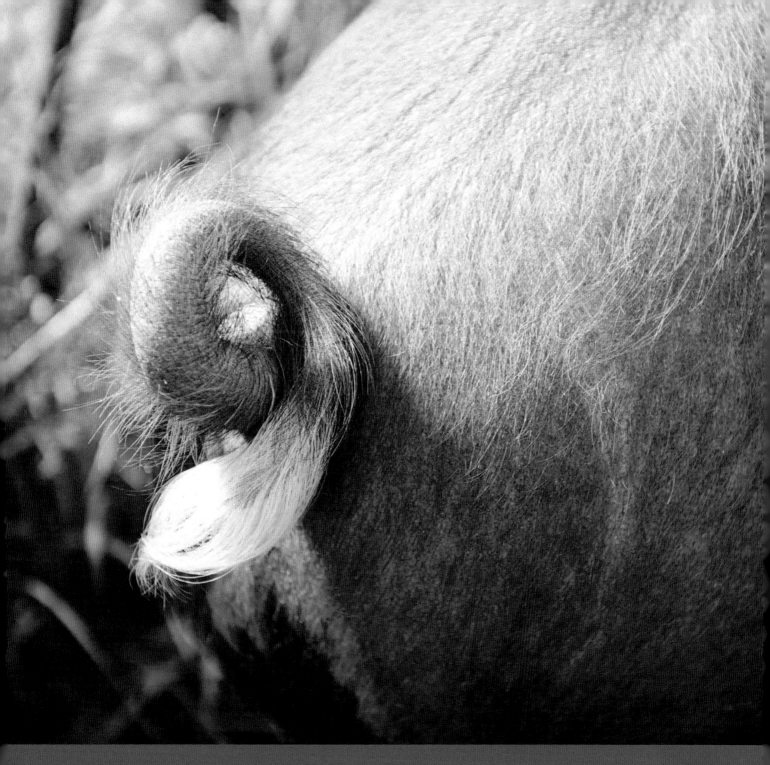

Epilogue

I hope this guide serves you well, and that you venture out on your own galactic pursuit of flavor and quality. Regardless of how far you step into a lifestyle of eating and drinking seasonally, I believe your perspective can be widened just by giving it some thought.

If we set all the technical specifics aside, my Beervangelism is centered on a few simple ideas.

Looking to the seasons and Mother Earth for inspiration will provide natural beauty, while also improving the quality and nutrition of our food and drink.

I firmly believe the appreciation of quality and flavor in our lives is one of the beautiful aspects of the human condition. We should not let apathy draw us away or limit us from the artistry we're capable of enjoying in this world. Those who care must rise up to champion quality and mindful producers in any way they can. We must do this, not for any individual producer's sake, but for humankind and future generations.

As people grow up and strike out on their own, they have important choices to make that will be influenced by what they've been exposed to. We must remember to show them a world that is wider than shrink-wrapped, pre-made food designed to fool our bodies and palates with fillers, preservatives, and high fructose corn syrup. I am careful not to judge, but I believe strongly that if young people are exposed to better options and shown the path, they'll naturally make more choices that are good for them. If they learn to enjoy shopping and cooking, their lives may change forever.

As much as we enjoy the fruits of our expertise and the treasures we find, we should remember that the greatest treat is to share food and drink with those we care about, generously and graciously.

I set out to write The Beervangelist's Guide to invite people on a journey, but I feel as if I was the one that took the trip. I'm eternally grateful for the path I discovered through the world of beer. As you can see, it connects to a much broader trail system with endless opportunities for intrigue and discovery.

I invite you to bring this lifestyle into your home for yourself. However, I believe that as we take these small steps, we are joining something larger, reconnecting communities, systems, and philosophies that will change the world.

As long as we care and believe that we as a people can do better, our world will be full of flavor, comfort, and nutrition. No matter where we are in the world or what we eat and drink, if we stop to recognize and appreciate the beauty of it all, we will undoubtedly live the good life.

Cheers!

About the Author

Fred Bueltmann, AKA the Beervangelist, is an owner of New Holland Brewing Company and nationally recognized expert on pairing beer and food. He is a Certified Cicerone®, past president of the Michigan Brewers Guild, and recipient of their prestigious "Tom Burns Award" recognizing the pioneering spirit of the "Great Beer State." Fred serves as a judge for the Brewers Association's Great American Beer Festival and authors "Beer and Food with the Beervangelist," a column in Michigan food magazines. Fred is an ardent advocate for quality food and craft beer's place at the table.

Fred and his wife Ulla live on their small horse farm amidst the rolling hills of Fennville, Michigan, with their many friendly critters.

Made in the USA
Lexington, KY
29 August 2013